Sharing the Crust

"An extended meditation on the challenges and joys of Christian discipleship, and on the mystery of self-surrender, *Sharing the Crust* does more than tell the story of a remarkable man and the community he guided in West Baltimore. Part memoir, part biography, part history, part prayer, this marvelous book provides a glimpse of what it is like to bring hope to the poor, and for making possible what is deemed impossible by many in the world. Truly inspiring and unforgettable."

—Carlos Eire, T. Lawrason Riggs Professor of History and Religious Studies, Yale University, National Book Award winner, *Waiting for Snow in Havana*

"If you sit down and really read *Sharing the Crust*, you will experience God's fullness. All of us in the story of faith that Mark tells were so different, but God brought us together, and we were of one accord. I'm thankful that I'm still living here in Sandtown, and I'm believing that God is going to do even more work here. For anyone embarking on grassroots ministry, read from those of us who went through it!"

—Nina Anderson, leader in Sandtown neighborhood of Baltimore

"Can pain, loss, and hope co-exist? Injustice, deprivation, and celebration? How does individual calling, communal vocation, the search for justice, and commitment to place relate? Mark Gornik's evocative ode to radical friendship and community building 'on the journey towards new creation' offers embodied and generative responses to such urgent questions. I could not put it down!"

—Ruth Padilla De Borst, associate professor of world Christianity, Western Theological Seminary

"Mark Gornik has written a remarkable story that responds to Peter's invitation to 'give an account' of hope. This story is a witness to another order, a fresh possibility, an alternative, a true and good radiance. In it, you will encounter and be changed by the faith and courage, the friendship and community that made it all possible. Read *Sharing the Crust* and see how God is always in the process of 'doing a new thing,' a 'new song,' in the wildernesses and deserts of our time."

—Fr. Emmanuel Katongole, co-founder and president, Bethany Land Institute, professor of theology, University of Notre Dame

"*Sharing the Crust* is an inspirational story interwoven in a theology of the reign of God that is in our midst. Reading it is to discover that the kingdom is within us and that all things are truly possible when we come to know each other and truly care. As you read, grow, and be transformed into the real people of God."

—Elizabeth Conde-Frazier, author of *Atando Cabos*

"Despite the cynicism about both church and state these days, *Sharing the Crust* testifies and demonstrates that things can change, hope can be rekindled, and faith can be restored with love, justice, and peacemaking. In this testament you will witness a Sacrament in Sandtown, the name of the place where this creative community was formed. This is not just a good read, but a good example that we all need."

—Jim Wallis, Archbishop Desmond Tutu Chair of Faith and Justice, Georgetown University

Sharing the Crust

A Communion of Saints in a Baltimore Neighborhood

MARK R. GORNIK

Foreword by JOHN M. PERKINS
Afterword by PETER B. PRICE

CASCADE *Books* • Eugene, Oregon

SHARING THE CRUST
A Communion of Saints in a Baltimore Neighborhood

Copyright © 2024 Mark R. Gornik. All rights reserved. Except for brief quotations in critical publications or reviews, no part of this book may be reproduced in any manner without prior written permission from the publisher. Write: Permissions, Wipf and Stock Publishers, 199 W. 8th Ave., Suite 3, Eugene, OR 97401.

Cascade Books
An Imprint of Wipf and Stock Publishers
199 W. 8th Ave., Suite 3
Eugene, OR 97401

www.wipfandstock.com

PAPERBACK ISBN: 978-1-6667-5352-3
HARDCOVER ISBN: 978-1-6667-5353-0
EBOOK ISBN: 978-1-6667-5354-7

Cataloguing-in-Publication data:

Names: Gornik, Mark R., author. | Foreword by John M. Perkins. | Afterword by Peter B. Price.
Title: Sharing the crust : a communion of saints in a Baltimore neighborhood / Mark R. Gornik; foreword by John M. Perkins; afterword by Peter B. Price.
Description: Eugene, OR: Cascade Books, 2024 | Includes bibliographical references.
Identifiers: ISBN 978-1-6667-5352-3 (paperback) | ISBN 978-1-6667-5353-0 (hardcover) | ISBN 978-1-6667-5354-7 (ebook)
Subjects: LCSH: Allan Tibbels, 1955–2010. | City churches—Baltimore—Maryland. | City missions—Baltimore—Maryland.
Classification: BV637 .G635 2024 (print) | BV637 (ebook)

The artwork on the cover, taken from the full piece found on page 168, is by Willa Bickham, with her granddaughter Julia Walsh-Little.

Unless otherwise indicated, the Scripture quotations in this publication are from The New Revised Standard Version.

To Rita, Peter, and Daniel
Reginald (Big Man), Jermaine, Kurt, and Mr. Kelley
in memory of LaVerne Stokes, Anton Holly, and Ella Johnson
and to Ike and Susan, for everything

Heaven is a banquet and life is a banquet, too,
even with a crust, where there is companionship.

—Dorothy Day, *The Long Loneliness*

Contents

Foreword—John M. Perkins xi

Stoop 1

Grace 4

Sunday 11

Wall 21

Prayer 28

Signs 34

Chess 41

Furniture 49

Circle 85

Crayons 93

Loaves 103

Birds 110

Three 119

Fire 129

Music 134

Paths 142

Time 146

Breath (Coda) 155

Afterword—Peter B. Price 161

Contents

Acknowledgments 164

Further Resources / Bibliography 169

Love (Daniel Berrigan—*Love, Love at the End*) 184

Foreword

The story in this book is of one of the joys of my life: a vision of a beloved community. It shows life together that Jesus wants built across the dividing lines of our world. That life together is one of community marked by mutuality of discipleship.

In *Sharing the Crust*, you will meet a community of Christians in a neighborhood in Baltimore who went beyond what Dietrich Bonhoeffer called "cheap grace." Allan Tibbels, his wife Susan, Jenny, Jessica, Jane, Ike, LaVerne, Antoine, Patty, Mike, Fitt, Nina, Gary, Orlando, Elder Harris, Mrs. Harris, and so many others, communicated God's love powerfully in how they lived and worked together.

I loved Allan, and we sought to understand one another. Allan wanted to live out the gospel as if his life depended on it—and he did, as did Susan, his family, and the entire community.

Allan was the real thing. He both embraced his own suffering and entered into the suffering of others. He took up the way of Jesus, the cross of suffering and reconciliation. He was committed to living out the gospel in a real community, and to seeing justice and nonviolence practiced—a commitment we all need. Allan's spirit and passion for Christ and for Sandtown live in this story. And it lives on in my own heart and story.

From Mark's first visit to Voice of Calvary in 1980 to the year he later spent living at Harambee House, our family and community are pleased to have been a part of his journey, and now of his life with Rita.

When Mark first invited me to Sandtown in 1988 to speak at the dedication of their church and ministry center, I came not knowing what to expect. But I loved it. Not only the neighbors, but local politicians like Mayor Kurt Schmoke and city council members and national figures from both major political parties, including the Democratic senator Paul Sarbanes and the Republican Department of Housing and Urban Development

(HUD) secretary Jack Kemp, and Dan Coats, then a Republican senator from Indiana, all attended and joined in the celebration.

Since that first visit, I have been with them at key moments throughout their history, returning often for house dedications, anniversaries, and then for Allan's funeral.

The kind of work they did in Sandtown was not easy, and community life is messy and painful. We are, after all, sinners. But this story also demonstrates something I have been speaking about my whole life: that only the gift of Christ, the blood of Christ, can truly begin to heal our divided and broken world. I need that gift and that healing. Each one of us needs God's grace and forgiveness as we watch for and participate in the new things God is doing all around us.

Sharing the Crust shows the power of Christ's love lived out in community. It shows why working for justice and human dignity matters. It shows why beginning at the community level, with the people of a neighborhood, is essential.

As I think about Allan and Susan, about Mark and everyone I know in Sandtown, I am not merely satisfied with its meaning and memory in my life. I am filled with joy and gratitude to God for its witness to the world.

Read this book by my friend, Mark, which helps us think things through better than any I know, and be inspired (as he puts it) to share your crust of bread.

May you find a way, as Allan did, to make love the final witness.

Dr. John M. Perkins
Jackson, Mississippi

John M. Perkins is the founder and president emeritus of the John and Vera Mae Perkins Foundation and the cofounder of the Christian Community Development Association. He recently completed his three-book "manifesto," One Blood: Parting Words to the Church on Race and Love; He Called Me Friend: The Healing Power of Friendship in a Lonely World; *and* Count It All Joy: The Ridiculous Paradox of Suffering. *The recipient of numerous awards, Perkins is recognized globally for his visionary and faithful leadership.*

Stoop

Morning belongs to North Mount Street at the corner of Laurens Street. To the Spirit of God who awakens and renews all creation. To the stoop.[1]

I am sitting on the Baltimore marble steps of my 1304 North Mount Street home, their features smoothed down by the imprint of feet across generations. Allan is in front of me on the sidewalk, leaning back and stretching his arms outward, then pressing downward on the arms of his wheelchair until he gets a slight lift off the cushion. We breathe in the morning air, still cool before the summer heat takes over, baking into the concrete.

Across the street, the sun begins to bathe the playground, swimming pool, and McAbee's basketball courts, our asphalt and brick-lined Central Park, but in West Baltimore and adjoined to the Gilmor Homes. Mr. Kelley runs the recreation center and is readying the pool. Soon it will be filled with kids jumping and splashing, staying cool, just as they were during the night, when a magical hole appears in the fence, inviting a late-at-night all neighborhood swim. That is, until the Foxtrot helicopter arrives out of the dark of night, and everyone scatters until the next night.

From this end of the block, we can see a long line of red brick row houses. Something like every other one is abandoned, their collapsed roofs, beams, and floors jutting out. Such ruins send out a message that they will either disappear or be revived, timetable unknown, possibilities still to unfold. The roof that remains is home to pigeon coops.

The Busy Bee sign is still visible across the street on Laurens. Just past the end of the block, across Lorman Street, is the Livelystone COGIC church, a cross posted outside on the upper floor, keeping vigil over the

---

1. "Morning does not belong to the individual; it belongs to all the church of the Triune God . . . ," Bonhoeffer, *Life Together and Prayerbook of the Bible*, 49.

neighborhood. Around the corner is the Freeloaders social club. Fox's is on the corner of Mount and Fulton, and over on Presstman is the Odyssey.

Here on the stoop, we are talking about the neighborhood, a book we read, Scripture, a prayer we offered, music, a film we want to see at the Charles, and sports, all at once. I am in my pastor's uniform of khakis, a button-down shirt, and black shoes. Allan is in his strict attire of black jeans, T-shirt, and black Adidas. He notes my unchanging style; I return the compliment.

A young Ike is now here, having just made the step from one stoop over. He is laughing with both Allan and me as we banter. How could he not! Happy to see Ike, Tungba, our church black lab, is barking in the window!

Fitt, Gary, Orlando, Lisa, Anton, Arteze, Damon, Shaconda, Tyra, Nita, and Luck find a place too as the steps fill up and then overflow. Frank finds his way here from Calhoun, and he asks where Miss Suzie is. On his way to work, Mac greets everyone, and Mamie leans out of the doorway, smiles, and lets us know she is there. Tick ambles by and goes around the corner; Richard, Raymond, Roland, and Mr. Charlie say hello. Mr. Holmes is sitting nearby on his stoop.

LaVerne pulls up in her car, beeps the horn, then pulls over and joins everyone. "Yeah yeah," she says, and greets everyone by name and with a smile. Nina is with her, and comes over to talk with Allan. Al is here too, and he is reminding us of work we have to do. Sonia arrives and invites everyone over for a plate of mac and cheese, best deal in Sandtown. Mr. "Ulysses" Carter, in suit and tie, adds his touch of stately dignity. Jane is here talking with Susan, Jenny, and Jessica. Miss Brightsy is in front, standing on the Word. Suzanne is here, and we are glad she is. Dr. Dave is here too. Janice is also here, and with her usual joy!

In front of us on Laurens Street, Reginald "Big Man" is Arabbing, guiding his horse-drawn cart down the street, peddling his fruits and vegetables. "Arabbing" is an African American trade in Baltimore of horse-drawn carts filled with fruits and vegetables for sale in neighborhoods without grocery stores.[2] Reginald comes over to say hello, to talk to Ike and Allan.

Thomas stops by, sharing a word with Allan, Ike, and others. A police car slows down, then speeds up through the stop sign, nary a glance our way. "Knockers," somebody remarks, as another car speeds by toward the Western district, past Morton's Funeral Home. "Five-O" too.

---

2. Freeman, *Arabbers of Baltimore*.

Ms. Carol is waving from up the block, Ms. Claudia from across the street. Antoine, Patty, and Mike are present, Mark, Ryan, Denise, Tamika, and Tyesha too. Riding his bike over is Elder Harris, looking good as usual!

Yes, there will be houses for us to build, alleyways to clean, a school for neighborhood children to open, laments to offer, brokenness to heal, forgiveness to seek, powers to be confronted, streets to be walked, bread to be shared, and trees and flowers to be planted.

What will take place in Sandtown will remind us of the book of Isaiah. Isaiah's world, like the world we knew, was marked by violence and division. What God was going to do was going to reshape a people to be a light, a peaceable presence. As this life drew people from all backgrounds, they would become a "mountain of the Lord's house." They would learn not just to put down their defenses and insecurities but turn their swords into plowshares. They would renounce war.[3] They will take up the struggle of the Servant of the Lord.[4]

Putting aside divisions and conflicts, in Sandtown we will learn to pick up the tools of peace like hammers and garden tools. And now in Baltimore, in a neighborhood known for sand, will be a mountain of the Lord's house.

But for now, on the stoop, we are young, absorbing energy from all around us—the sun and streets, one another. Our defenses are down; there is laughter and joy, light and love. Ordinary life. Blessed life. Gentle life. Fragile and tender life. A life of gratitude for the little things. Life freely lived together as it is intended to be. We are home, life as God intends for all of creation.

Like a fresco etched across rows of houses in the neighborhood, we can see God's new city is bursting forth. We can hear the bells of Jubilee ringing, pealing across the streets of Sandtown, and look to a promised day when all will be made right, when we will return home from exile, sisters and brothers, together.[5]

Can you see God's new city bursting forth? Can you hear the bells of Jubilee ringing?

---

3. Isaiah 2; Lohfink, *Jesus and Community*, 170–76. My thanks to Steve Fowl for this reading.

4. Isaiah 52–53.

5. This image comes from Bruce Cockburn, "Santiago Dawn." See also the book of Haggai, and the return of the exiles.

Grace

"Allan died." This is all I say, words of loss and pain nearly bursting out. Silence holds the air, and then Sister Grace says quite directly and simply, "Allan is with you." I ask her to say more. After a few moments, Sister Grace repeats the same words. "Allan is with you." I take it in, holding it without more words between us.

Boarding the Metro-North train at the 125th Street station in Harlem, I settle into my seat, following along with the rhythms of the Hudson River. I am on my way to Maryknoll, the headquarters of the Catholic religious order of the same name. I am on my way to visit Sister Grace.

Allan's funeral is now only a few weeks past, and my mind is filled with memories. Putting his understanding of the gospel into practice, Allan with his family moved to the West Baltimore neighborhood called Sandtown, where he stayed for the rest of his life, working tirelessly for justice and peace. He did so with a love for his neighbors, a life devoted to prayer, and an uncanny sense of comic timing. If Allan helped build houses, he was really building community, showing us how to care for one another over time, how to love our neighbor. He was showing us what mattered.

I know this because the entire course of my ministry was in fellowship with Allan. To use a phrase of Daniel Berrigan's, the Jesuit priest, peace activist, and poet whom, with his brother Philip Berrigan, Allan admired greatly, we shared a "vision of great work to be done."[1] This vision is the kingdom of God, peace, justice, reconciliation and joy in the Holy Spirit. To live this gospel imperative, we shared what we had, and then stayed with one another.[2]

---

1. Berrigan, *Mission*, 125.
2. Luke 10:1–9.

GRACE

The first thing I always see when arriving at Maryknoll is the grand fieldstone seminary building and chapel, its tower, roof, and columns built to convey an image of China from a century ago, where and when Maryknoll began its vocation. Sister Grace resides in the Chalet, a small house across the street from the seminary, part of the Contemplative Community of Maryknoll Sisters. Together they live a life of prayer.

The Maryknoll Sisters, like the Maryknoll Brothers and Fathers, have an active spirit to live with and serve the poor around the world, originally in China, then Korea, and more recently in places like El Salvador and East Africa.[3] When I step foot on Maryknoll grounds, I know the Spirit and this spirit is real and runs deep.

Born and raised in New York City, in the borough of Queens, Sister Grace has been a Maryknoll Sister for over fifty years. She holds close the world as overflowing with the energies of Love, of Christ. For a decade, Sister Grace has walked with me on my journey. To discern where I am with God, and where God is with me on my journey, I travel to Maryknoll a few times each year to be in conversation with Sister Grace, and we have spoken often about Allan, about Sandtown.

As Sister Grace and I talked further that day, about what it means that Allan is with me, she conveyed an awareness of how God's Love is a way of understanding our world, and who we are to one another. In a beautiful way, she described that we are woven together in life, in beauty, in truth. A belonging, a communion, rooted in Love. Communion is our presence, our service, our stories, alive in Love. Communion is all we have. Communion is all we need.

When someone close to us dies, it can move us to think more deeply not only about human significance and existence, but about who we are to one another. When Allan died, I thought about all the relationships that flowed through him. As Haitian-American novelist Edwidge Danticat helps us to see and feel in *Brother, I'm Dying*,[4] death is about our stories, our memories, the fragility of our human bonds, our losses, and our fears. As Danticat also observes in *The Art of Death: Writing the Final Story*, a book on the death of her mother and others near to her, a particular death can also lead us to reflect on death and loss on a wider scale.[5]

---

3. Lernoux et al., *Hearts on Fire*.
4. Danticat, *Brother, I'm Dying*.
5. Danticat, *Art of Death*.

Sharing the Crust

Family losses, the catastrophes of our world: she—we—try to make sense of our world and its losses. Writing helps Danticat to see and name reality more closely. It helps us to see as well, to become more attentive to pain and suffering, to injustices that claim lives in our neighborhoods, cities, and world, and to know a love that overcomes death, bonds of belonging that are not lost.

On the train home from Maryknoll, as I thought about Allan, Sandtown, and the life we shared, about what Sister Grace said, and the questions I now had, my mind turned reflexively to the phrase "the communion of saints," found in the ancient Apostles' Creed.

We may not always take note of its full meaning and depth, but when Christians around the world voice the Apostles' Creed, we proclaim not only our belief about God, but how we believe God sees us, and how we are to see the world and one another.[6] The concluding of its three sections reads,

> I believe in the Holy Spirit,
> the holy catholic church,
> the communion of saints,
> the forgiveness of sins,
> the resurrection of the body,
> and the life everlasting. Amen.

These words name and can help shape a people who gather up all that is broken and divided. A community who receives forgiveness from God and one another. The Spirit of Christ who raises from the dead, bringing to life everlasting. A communion of saints among the company of heaven.

Allan, Sandtown, this reality of relationships is essential. "The very purpose of our being," writes the renowned historian and Orthodox Christian Albert Raboteau, "is to commune with others—to commune with the Divine Persons of the Holy Trinity, Father, Son, and Holy Spirit, and to commune with our fellow human persons."[7]

If I am truly with myself, I am with others and God, a wholeness of being, a communion, and with all creation. Indeed, we are created for friendship and love. It is this dwelling together that is a sacrament, an overflowing love as communion. "I do not call you servants any longer, because the servant does not know what the master is doing; but I have called you

---

6. On the creed, and the reasons for including this phrase and my general argument, see Lash, *Believing Three Ways*, 83–120 and Williams, *Tokens of Trust*, 101–2.

7. Raboteau, "American Salvation."

friends," Jesus proclaimed. Jesus dwells in God, and as we abide in God, and with one another, a communion occurs called friendship (John 17:23–26).

As the Catholic theologian Elizabeth Johnson stresses, the communion of saints is a not a theology or activity for the few, or one tradition, or just from the past. Instead, it is a theology for the whole people of God speaking up and living for justice and mercy in the here and now.[8]

The communion of saints is close to the African (and global) sense of being related to one another, to the ancestors through the living Christ. As the theologian John Mbiti reminds us, the biblical story is far bigger than we often imagine, and includes the children of Israel, the God of Abraham and Sarah, Isaac, and Jacob.[9] Here are ancestors who have gone before us, what the Letter to the Hebrews calls the "cloud of witnesses." They show us the way of faith.

The cloud includes prophets, saints, and witnesses who have heard the call to be human, to travel in the way of the beatitudes—of peacemaking, gentleness, love, steadfastness, and commitment. With their lives they have translated the gospel into a time and place, showing, inviting, and encouraging our fidelity to the gospel in our times and places. Through their example, they help us discover friendship with God and one another, a gift and sacrament of vulnerability. As Rowan Williams observes, such saints don't make human sense: they only make sense because of God.[10]

I wonder: Is the loss of a world of saints in much of the West a reason why so many find an encounter with God such a particular challenge?[11] Is it the saints, and the ancestors, who we need to open the door to God in a "secular age"? To our relationship to the land, to the places and communities where we belong? In our broken world, it may not be programs or plans we need, but saints, witnesses, and prophets who point to faith, beauty, and justice, to the meaning of the gospel as the fullness of life.

Saints point us to our need for God and one another. "We stand not alone, as solitary individual selves," writes Raboteau,

> but in compassionate solidarity with others, the saints, who have gone before, our ancestors in the faith, whose icons surround us at church and at home—a cloud of living witnesses. And we stand

8. Johnson, *Friends of God and Prophets*.

9. Mbiti, *New Testament Eschatology in an African Background*.

10. Williams, *Luminaries*; *Tokens of Trust*; "Religious Lives." For elaboration, see Hagman, "Saints in Public."

11. Taylor, *Secular Age*; Brown, *Cult of the Saints*. See also Eire, *Reformations*.

in solidarity with our brothers and sisters in the present, especially with those who suffer.[12]

They give us examples of holy lives, solidarity, care, and responsibility.

The epigraph, and the inspiration for the title of this book, is taken from Dorothy Day's memoir, *The Long Loneliness*.

> We cannot love God unless we love each other and to love we must know each other. We know Him in the breaking of bread, and we know each other in the breaking of bread, and we are not alone any more. Heaven is a banquet and life is a banquet, too, even with a crust, where there is companionship.[13]

Centered in love for God and neighbor, in sharing with and learning about one another in the breaking of bread, in Christ, in the gift of an eternal festive joy, Day provides us with as compelling of a summary of Christian faith that I know.

Ours is an age where it matters acutely how we belong to one another. How do we share in a world of bodies? With whom do we share? Are we prepared to think and live differently if we are formed by the Eucharist, Jesus as the bread of life? How do we now share that bread, even the smallest of pieces, the crust, that we hold? And how do we share not only with friends, but also with enemies? Christian faith is an invitation to take up the call in 1 Corinthians 11:23–25 to remember Christ in a meal, his "body for you." In the meal we share, in the life we are given, we look to Jesus, who proclaimed, "I am the bread of life."

Being in the middle of difficult things in Sandtown—race, class, place, history—I recognize that can be hard, not easy to understand, a challenge, then and now. Our life together as a community, and specifically Allan's life, was a risk; it was not easy or safe for any of us, especially since our life together did not fit easily into how we do or speak about "church" or "city." Allan's story, and the story of our community in Sandtown, was certainly about being in the middle of difficult things.

We didn't get it all right. Hardly! But we sought to be responsible, to hear and live the Word of God, to share our crust of bread. In the concrete action of responsibility, as Dietrich Bonhoeffer explained, it is inevitable that we do not get it all right. He writes:

---

12. Raboteau, "American Salvation."
13. Day, *Long Loneliness*.

GRACE

> If one has completely renounced making something of oneself—whether it be a saint or a converted sinner or a church leader (a so-called priestly figure!), a just or an unjust person, a sick or a healthy person—then one throws oneself completely into the arms of God, and this is what I call this-worldliness: living fully in the midst of life's tasks, questions, successes and failures, experiences, and perplexities—then one takes seriously no longer one's own sufferings but rather the sufferings of God in the world. Then one stays awake with Christ in Gethsemane.[14]

In the middle of things is where Allan, and each one of us, found ourselves, and therefore we needed the mercy of God. Sandtown was our school of faith.

In thinking about the loss of Allan, and other losses in Sandtown, I have been greatly moved by William Stringfellow, a Harvard-trained lawyer and theologian who lived and worked in East Harlem for a period of his life, and found theology in biography, in the Word lived out, in stories of faith that are parables. During his life, Stringfellow wrote profoundly about the Gospel as freedom from the power of death, the new life of the resurrection, and a life and politics that reflect this way of understanding the world and humanity.

In *A Simplicity of Faith*, Stringfellow responds to the loss of his friend and companion, Anthony Towne, and considers his own declining personal health and mortality, with both grief and mourning. *Grief*, Stringfellow observed, is a more immediate response to death of loss, anger, and bereavement. But *mourning*, he found, can be expressed through "the liturgies of recollection, memorial, affection, honor, gratitude, confession, empathy, intercession, meditation, anticipation for the life of the one who is dead."[15]

Sharing the Crust is a prayer. And I offer this prayer as a liturgy of recollection, hope, confession, gratitude, a meditation on friendship and communion. In the way that Stringfellow describes, it is about my experience of the loss of Allan and others, and a theological description of a life in God, theology through biography. And in the midst of this experience of grief and mourning, somehow, I know as the Canadian musician and singer Bruce Cockburn sang, that "joy will find a way."[16]

---

14. Bonhoeffer, *Letters and Papers from Prison*, 486. See also Bonhoeffer, *Ethics*.
15. Stringfellow, *Simplicity of Faith*, 22.
16. Cockburn, "Joy Will Find a Way."

Sharing the Crust

To tell this story, I have drawn on conversations, personal notebooks, journals, newspaper articles, photographs, music, and a trove of documentary materials. I have also reread books and articles that were important to Allan, to us, and I read new materials on cities and community that speak to Sandtown.[17] But most of all, I have sought to stay close to our experience, and to give an account of faith.

There is, of course, more than one Sandtown story, more than one way to tell this story, and more than one way to see the light of grace reflected in all its beauty and hard edges. But the only way I can tell this story, at this time, is through friendship and love, a parable of the upside-down reign of God.

Something unique, almost indescribable took place in Allan's life, in Sandtown, in a community. A social love lived out, a different type of politics and theology, the mystery of God's saving grace and justice, the experience of the reconciling work of Christ, lived out on a few blocks. While I don't fully know or understand our story, it is an experience that I know to be true. In a world of expanse where "Spacetime strings bend/ World without end," as Bruce Cockburn sings in an achingly beautiful song "To Fit in My Heart," I know our story yet fits in my heart.[18]

When Allan died, I knew I would write about his life, its witness and power, his own brokenness. Over time, it became clear this was not just a book about Allan, or our friendship, or even about New Song. It is about carrying the question that I asked Sister Grace, "What does it mean that Allan is with me?" And what does this mean for our understanding of the self, God, our relationship to one another, and with all of creation?

Sister Grace is right. *Communion is everything—we are woven together in life, in beauty, in truth. Belonging, communion rooted in Love. Our presence, our service, our stories, alive in Love. Communion is all we have. Communion is all we need.*

---

17. I look forward to continuing work on a project and archive that I hope will share and hold many more Sandtown stories and memories. See also my earlier work on Sandtown, Gornik, *To Live in Peace*.

18. Bruce Cockburn, "To Fit in My Heart."

Sunday

John Perkins looked like a biblical prophet, maybe Amos. As I would learn, John Perkins was not just a prophet, but an evangelist, community organizer, ministry developer, Bible teacher, and civil rights leader.

I first encountered John Perkins when, around age seventeen, visiting a now long closed Christian bookstore and coffee house in Baltimore, I came across *Let Justice Roll Down* displayed on one of those old metal spinning book racks.[1] From the cover, Perkins's visage looked at me, matching the words of the title about justice, drawn from the book of Amos. He certainly had a prophet's look of purpose and calling. I didn't need to leaf through the pages to know it was a book I had to read.

Let Justice Roll Down is the story of John Perkins, who in 1930 was born in New Hebron, Mississippi, a place of sharecrop farming and racial lines and oppression unbroken. His mother died of malnutrition a few months after John's birth; his father had left shortly after his birth. When his brother Clyde, returning from military service during World War II, was profiled, shot, and murdered by the deputy marshall in their hometown, dying in John's arms on the long trip to a hospital in Jackson that would treat a Black man, enough was enough. It was an easy move to California for John in 1947.

Perkins did not have to look back. But, on hearing a call from God, he did more than that: he moved back to Mississippi with his wife, Vera Mae, and their young family, living "across the tracks," this time in Mendenhall.

John, Vera Mae, and the whole Perkins family helped to begin a church and ministry called Voice of Calvary. With time, their work encompassed a day care program, cooperative farming, a legal clinic, and a church. Voice of Calvary began drawing volunteers from around the country to this distant

---

1. Perkins, *Let Justice Roll Down*.

patch of Mississippi. It was, however, the 1960s, and the threat of violence, even death, against African Americans and civil rights workers was always but a moment away in Mississippi.

One day, John was arrested and put in jail, where white jailers beat and tortured him almost to death. Released and alive only because the community organized, protested, and demanded it, he went to receive treatment and recover at the Mound Bayou Health Center. Here, John heard Christ bidding him to forgiveness and the work of reconciliation. And that's what he did, living a radical vision of Christianity that welcomed everyone to the table of God's kingdom.

I needed to learn more, so a few years later, in the summer of 1980, I went to Voice of Calvary, to attend their Jubilee Conference in Jackson, Mississippi. Here I heard about and saw the practical message of community-based development, health care, legal services, and cooperative economics fleshed out through the local church. Through Perkins's story and vision, I was being introduced to a vision for the body of Christ to "come alive in neighborhoods," as he wrote in the dedication to *A Quiet Revolution*.[2]

In Jackson and elsewhere—like the Sojourners Community in Washington, DC, where I visited and stayed for a few days before college—I was becoming aware of new visions of church and community in the city. I was also getting to know about Church of the Saviour in Washington, DC, that was doing very creative work developing small faith communities and ministries from a place of prayer.

In the places I was visiting, I could see what could happen when people take risks in response to the invitation of the Spirit and unleash new energies to envision, build, and sustain health centers, housing initiatives, community centers, and schools. It was hard to see how one could do the work of justice and peace without community. This realization opened my eyes not just to the communal focus of the Scriptures, including the New Testament churches, letters, and Gospels, but to community as the reality of the gospel. When I hear "Jesus is our peace" in Ephesians 2, I think of this new reality.

In what I can only attribute to the movement of the Spirit, by the age of eighteen, I was being drawn toward ministry, called in particular to the strand of Christian tradition that understands the city, its noises, flurry of

---

2. Perkins, *Quiet Revolution*. On Perkins's vision within American Christianity, see the landmark study by Marsh, *Beloved Community*.

Sunday

activities, frictions, and differences as also being the place of God's presence and ministry. Of a church on the ground, in community.

Reading Scripture was central in this course of life direction. Everywhere in the Old Testament, or the Hebrew Bible, I met God's commitment to and God's watch over the poor, the command to welcome the immigrant and stranger, and the call to care about just ways of living and organizing our lives. In the Gospels I encountered Jesus, who called us to a lifestyle of peacemaking, love, and nonviolence, the upside-down ways of the Beatitudes and the Sermon on the Mount. And from Genesis, Psalms, and the whole of Scripture, I found a connection between the choices we make and the future for all of creation and creatures.[3] I could see all of this lived out in the life of John Perkins.

During a year between high school and college, not long after I first learned about John Perkins and Voice of Calvary, I held a job as a laborer at a construction company. I had no idea what I was doing on a construction site, so my job was to fill in wherever I was needed. Soon a work assignment took me to the Maryland Training School, more recently renamed the Hickey School, a detention center, a prison really, a facility for young men set up outside Baltimore city.[4]

Here I saw groups of young men, many of them African American and nearly my age, being marched back and forth between buildings, locked up for meals or classes, and then walked back in a line to the "unit" in which they slept.

After telling some friends involved in youth ministry what I'd seen, we approached the Training School administration and received permission to visit one of the units on a weekly basis. Each week, and sometimes more than once a week, we went to the unit, pulling together skits that made us all laugh, singing songs, learning together in Bible study, but mostly simply talking together, finding ways to laugh and share our lives. Small acts of solidarity and friendship created together.

One of the young men I got to know was from West Baltimore, and as he and I spent time together, and with others as well, I heard about the challenges facing African American young men in Baltimore as they tried to grow up.

---

3. Finnerty, *No More Plastic Jesus*.

4. For background on youth prisons like the Training School, see Hager, "There Are Still 80 'Youth Prisons.'"

I knew enough to make an immediate comparison: we were from the same time zone and nation, but different worlds. Where I grew up, my zip code shaped how I was able to work here yet leave at the end of the day while young men equal in age are lined up, staying as prisoners. Being at the Training School prompted me to ask why this place of incarceration was even here in the first place. I was being confronted by the role of race and place in society, in my life and church, on the ground, in everything. And I started to rethink my faith.

If faith had been passed on from my parents, a recognition of my own culture and my own need for a new spirit, a new direction with Jesus at the center of my life, was also required. Conversion was not only a single point in time, but a lifelong process of asking my own questions, hearing the Word, seeing reality with new eyes, and seeking to live in the light of the reign of God. To begin to know the heart of Jesus.

Starting with *Before the Mayflower* by Lerone Bennett Jr., I began reading African American history.[5] And a few years later, as I was learning even more about the civil rights movement, I would encounter Vincent Harding's *There Is a River*, a story of a people seeking freedom and justice.[6] The civil rights movement's scope was comprehensive, as I would also read in the Baltimore writer Taylor Branch's trilogy of volumes about America during the King years.[7] I also turned to literature, and Ralph Ellison's *Invisible Man* pressed me to ask: What did I see? Who did I not see?

As I was learning the history, the inheritance I shared but had not learned in church or school, I was beginning to recognize that the American story, and much of Western Christianity—in other words, my story—often upheld if not created, overlooked, and then continued along racial lines.[8] Going back nearly four centuries, the history was about families torn apart, about the Middle Passage by ship across the Atlantic, about two hundred and fifty years of chattel slavery, the auction block, the cruelty and torture, the economic exploitation. When I read Toni Morrison's *Beloved* that engaged this history, I was overwhelmed by the pain she described, but also recognized that there was something more and different to see and hear, a bigger and more spiritual world that cried out against injustice.

---

5. Bennett Jr., *Before the Mayflower.*
6. Harding, *There is a River.*
7. Branch, *Parting the Waters* and subsequent volumes.
8. Carter, *Race.*

Sunday

What the scholar Christina Sharpe calls "the wake" followed—the aftermaths of slavery and racism in lynching, Jim Crow laws, sharecropping, urban segregation, the new Jim Crow of mass incarceration like the Training School, and attacks on Black churches—all matters that threatened Black being and existence.[9]

Not by accident of nature, I came to understand, had the white evangelical churches in which I had grown up relocated to the outermost reaches of the suburbs, ordering a different politics, expanding sprawl, leaving a large carbon footprint. By moving away from changing urban neighborhoods, they, we, were not just following lines of division between city and suburb, Black and white, but making the lines of segregation, and injustice, more indelible.

The more people left the city, like my family and home church, the greater the disinvestment in the city in basic infrastructure and common public goods, like transportation, libraries, fire departments, water pipes, public education. This not only broke the city but led to a more racially and economically divided region and state, the opposite of solidarity and community. And it is why, I was seeing, matters of economic and racial justice in America are never just simply individual choices, but embedded in a political economy, in forces that were determinative for neighborhoods and the urban future.

Pressed by what I was coming to learn, I was now asking whether there was a contradiction between the church life that I had known and that had left the city and Christian faith as represented in African American churches that I was learning about. In the life, preaching, and worship of Black churches with names and histories new to me, like the Church of God in Christ or COGIC, AME Zion, Baptist, and Spirit Filling Stations storefronts, I found a counter-testimony to all I had known. Here was a church that stayed in the city. It wasn't "sociological," but the gospel proclaimed, heard, and lived as good news for hearts and communities.[10]

A few summers later I began to read the theologian James Cone, starting with *God of the Oppressed*.[11] Theology, Cone said, had to begin and stay with the Black experience, and with God who is with the oppressed. To get

---

9. Sharpe, *In the Wake*.

10. For places to start, see Lincoln and Mamiya, *Black Church*; Spillers, "Fabrics of History"; Raboteau, *Slave Religion*; and McCaulley, *Reading While Black*.

11. Cone, *God of the Oppressed*. See also his *Martin and Malcolm*, *Cross and the Lynching Tree*, and *Said I Wasn't Gonna Tell Nobody*. For background, see Daymond et al., eds., *T&T Clark Handbook of African American Theology*.

here, Cone identified the prophetic nature of Scripture, introduced Black theology, and pressed more questions about the meaning of Christian faith, church, and power. The cross was a lynching tree (as Cone named the locus of Christian theology), a symbol in a world marked by the racism, systemic violence, and the terror of white supremacy.

Could I hear the cries of blood in the soil, Cone asked the church—me? Such questions urged new ways of seeing, thinking, and living that became central to how I understood the Christian story. Cone, Perkins, and many others were shining the light of Christian truth, the possibility of a liberating faith, on a broken world, and calling the church to be a different community.

It was just a few years earlier that Allan and I met. Let it be stipulated that the first time we met it was at church, and neither Allan, nor Susan, nor I wanted to be there. Let the irony also be named that it was a white church in the suburbs of Baltimore. The year was 1977. I was sixteen, Allan and Susan each twenty-two. We couldn't possibly see it then, but our lives would never be the same after that encounter.

The congregation had relocated from a historic sanctuary in a lovely Baltimore neighborhood to a suburban plot of land next to the beltway that cut off the city. My family had been among those who had left the city and then joined the new church. I can still smell the scent of the newly poured concrete slab and vinyl-sided prefab building, feel the gravel in the church parking lot where I learned to drive my parents' car, and hear the scrum of cars through the high fence that divided the church from the beltway.

I was in high school and had other plans for that evening. But my parents, who had held me as an infant, prayed for me over the years, cared for me always, insisted: "Just go and meet the new youth leaders." Turns out that Allan and Susan, these very new youth leaders, had to be talked into going, too.

Hey, I'm Allan, he says as he introduces himself to me. To which, in reply, I say as little as possible. Maybe I said, *Hey, I'm Mark.* Or *Sure. Great. Got it.* Or something like that. And Susan with those tennis shoes: Please! I don't recall anything else that was said in the youth group meeting, but I do remember that afterwards Allan invited me to meet later at a local video arcade. No agenda, no follow-up questions, no lectures about the challenges facing a teenager, just playing pinball, shooting a game of pool, and talking about what was in our album collections. I learned Allan was big on the Stones.

Sunday

While at the time Allan and I did not know the book *The Suburban Captivity of the Churches*, written in 1961,[12] from music to dress to religious expectations to questions of the day we recognized that our local church tracked very closely to a specific suburban cultural identity and social location that went largely unacknowledged. It was an early introduction to the gospel and culture!

I was impressed that at other times Allan and Susan welcomed me into their home along with other kids from the youth group. I even went to my first and only "ice cream social" with the youth group. As Susan would remind me more than once years later after I became her pastor, she had wondered what my chances were. Not great, she concluded. All respect to Susan!

Looking back, I remember not just Susan's organizing skills, but her ministry, leadership, and pastoral life. And in Allan, I recognize how he sought to make others feel important and uniquely significant. Allan saw God's gifts in others, and in his own way trusted what God was doing, urging people along as he saw possibilities.

I can see how God used their gifts together then, and this would only grow.

Allan was born and raised in the suburbs of Baltimore. For the middle child of three brothers, his parents Mel and Marie provided a stable, working-class environment. Allan and Susan met in high school and, after graduation, at the age of eighteen, they married, planning for a life of wealth and material success. Right to work they went, starting off with a franchised cleaning company, while also becoming more involved in youth ministry.

On their way to achieving their dreams of success, something changed for Allan and Susan; a calling to turn in a different direction captured their imaginations. In order to work full time with Youth for Christ, a national Christian youth ministry focused on unchurched youth, they sold their business and gave away much of what they had. But first, in the months before moving and their new job starting, they began attending this church, the same one as my family. The pastor spotted them in the pews and persuaded Allan and Susan to accept a temporary assignment to lead the youth group.

Soon enough, as anticipated, Allan and Susan left the church and youth group to work full-time in youth ministry, moving to Columbia, a

---

12. Winter, *Suburban Captivity*. My thanks to John Wimmer for reminding me of this book.

planned community closer to Washington. We stayed in touch, and Allan wrote me a college recommendation.

In that same summer of 1980, before leaving Baltimore to begin college, and with a range of faith experiences giving me new questions and hopes, I joined Allan and a group of friends on a canoe trip to the Boundary Waters of Minnesota and Canada. Gliding across the clearest of lakes amidst beautiful forests, Allan and I shared a canoe, caught fresh fish every day for dinner, and had a running conversation about our faith, the church, and the world.

Allan was also moving in similar directions to me, seeking to understand the gospel as bigger and more socially engaged than we had previously understood. In the canoe, we talked about Scripture, the Anabaptist peace tradition, John Perkins and Voice of Calvary, the British evangelical John Stott, C. René Padilla in Latin America, Ron Sider in Philadelphia, the Chicago Declaration, Bread for the World, *The Other Side*, and Black prophetic voices such as those of Bill Pannell and Tom Skinner. And we were particularly moved by *Sojourners* magazine and its editor Jim Wallis, who wrote *Agenda for Biblical People* and *Call to Conversion*.

These Christian leaders, pastors and publications, and many others, exhibited deep biblical roots, and they had a universal and global concern, rather than merely an American outlook. They were calling the West, and the churches of the West, to a new way of a deeper biblical faith. Together, the range and shared clarity of these voices and communities represented what felt truly hopeful time for American evangelicalism, an opportunity for change, forward movement in areas of race, the environment, justice, public thought, the leadership of women in the church.[13]

While recognizing there is a wide range of traditions and streams within American evangelicalism,[14] in the window of those years we genuinely believed the overall trajectory of this tradition could take a new and forward course.[15] There was a movement toward what the missiologist Wilbert Shenk called the "whole gospel," a view of God's reign that moves beyond either/or choices.[16]

---

13. The literature is vast, but on this historical period I still find helpful Fowler, *New Engagement*.

14. For an introduction to more strands of evangelicalism, including holiness and revival movements, see Dayton, *Discovering an Evangelical Heritage*.

15. For a different view, see Sharp, *Other Evangelicals*.

16. Shenk, "Whole is Greater."

However, by the mid-1980s, the transformation we thought was possible for American evangelicalism was gone. Instead, conservative politics became meshed with a religious vision, an outlook adopted in the public media. By contrast, we believed what was needed was not a Christian Left to the Christian Right version of America, or even a third way that borrowed from both parties, but a biblical radicalism that grounded a different vision of humanity and community. The political challenge, as William Stringfellow emphasized, was to live humanly, to resist the powers of death, to live in fidelity to the power of the resurrection.[17]

Now decades from that time, American evangelicalism is where it is, with a similar range of problems and dissenting counter voices, as if on repeat, but much the worse for wear.[18] Many will wonder, can this spiral be broken, or is there another path coming to be?

Though Allan went home to the birth of his daughter Jessica, and I began my freshman year at Covenant College, a small Christian school in the south, upon parting ways at the end of the canoe trip, we shared an understanding that one day we might well do something together in Baltimore. Whatever concerns and criticisms Allan and I shared about church as we knew it, we shared a love for Christ's body, and a commitment to serve and be involved in building up the local church. Hope and enthusiasm were moving us.

Over the years, I often think about what would have happened if I hadn't stopped in that bookstore and been introduced to John Perkins and Voice of Calvary, if my parents had not urged me to go to youth group and prayed continually for me, if Susan and Allan had not been passing through and accepted the pastor's request to lead a youth group, if Allan had not reached out to me to befriend me, if I had not worked at a construction company and ended up working at a youth prison, if we had not ended up together on that canoe trip.

Allan, I now know, wondered too. As he and Susan wrapped up their time as youth leaders in the church where we first met, on June 14, 1978, he mused in his journal, "We're not understanding as to why God would have us develop these relationships when we know we'll be moving on."

Our world is a place of continual interactions and implications. Who is to know the impact of our words, the decisions we make, the importance

---

17. Stringfellow, *Ethic for Christians and Other Aliens in a Strange Land*.
18. For assessments, see Butler, *White Evangelical Racism*; Tisby, *Color of Compromise*.

of a single meeting, the time and attentiveness we give to the people we encounter?

I know a holy mystery that I can only grasp in the smallest of parts: that God, the creator of heaven and earth, is Love, and that all of existence and our relationships exist in this Love. Because God's Love is in and before all things, our response to God is not one that can be managed but is to be lived moment by moment, freely, attentively, and responsively.[19]

And remember *this* mystery, too: You never know what might happen when you attend a church youth group meeting!

We are Sunday's children.

---

19. Williams, *Tokens of Trust*, 31–55.

Wall

One spring morning, May 27, 1981, Allan got up, dressed for basketball, said goodbye to his Susan, and headed off to the church gym for a pick-up game. He couldn't wait.

Allan loved basketball. He loved the NBA, his favorite team the New York Knicks, and of course the NBA Finals, but Allan especially loved playing. He loved joining with friends, staff, and students from the youth ministry where he worked, running up and down the court, leaving nothing behind, giving his all to win.

This game underway, Allan started in on a lay-up, his feet going up into the air. But instead of landing on his feet and the shot dropping down through the net, his legs tangled up beneath him. Allan's body, his head first, was now in full and direct flight toward the wall on which the backboard was braced. The wall did not move or bend.

Allan crumpled down on the gym floor, a complete stillness overtaking his body. His neck was broken, his spinal cord was irreparably severed. Sunk down into a world of physical unfeeling, Allan knew immediately that he would never walk again. He was twenty-six years of age, with a wife and two young daughters.

News of Allan's injury reaches me a few days later when the pay phone rings on my college dormitory floor. "It's for you," says the person who knocks on my door.

The call is from Gary, Allan's brother. He tells me about the basketball game, that a helicopter evacuated Allan from a local hospital to the Shock Trauma center in Baltimore, and that they are working to save his life. Allan will likely live, Gary says, but he will be paralyzed from the neck down, his legs and body no longer working as they should. He is not expected to walk again.

Allan suffered a C6/C7 compression fracture of his vertebrae, becoming a quadriplegic, paralyzed, without feeling from his upper chest down. Spinal cord injuries vary. This level of severe spinal injury meant that while Allan retained some motion of his arms, but no more than the capacity to curl his fingers, he had also lost control of his legs, and of his bowel and bladder functions. Breathing was now difficult because the muscles needed to expand and contract his lungs did not work properly. Moving about would require the assistance of an electric wheelchair.

In Baltimore, the story of Joni Eareckson, a young woman who broke her neck in a diving accident, rendering her quadriplegic, was well known and respected. Joni had been a Baltimore area resident at the time of her injury, and both her Christian faith and the scope of her hardships were familiar to Allan.[1] From Joni's story, Allan knew his journey ahead would be filled with suffering and spiritual challenges.

The "wall." The "chair." These two words now become the shorthand Allan adopts, as in, "I hit the wall" and my body now depends on being in an electric wheel "chair." They are words that mark the disruption that comes with his severe trauma, about having your life undone.

On the day he broke his neck, Susan found that Allan had written down on a piece of paper these words from the book of Job: "Though he slay me, yet will I trust him" (13:15). Allan believed God was not only in charge of things, but that at the center of God's care for him was Love. And Love is Trust.

"God is sovereign," Allan said almost daily throughout his life, especially after he hit the wall.

Allan did not believe either in "accidents" or a capricious God, nor did he place responsibility for his injury upon God or cease believing in God. Nor did he look for or accept easy answers in matters of suffering. Instead, he placed his story in a larger story of God's providential care for creation, for his life.[2] But it was also personal, and Allan believed with Jeremiah that, "the way of human beings is not in their control, that mortals as they walk cannot direct their steps" (Jeremiah 10:23). He felt this was as far as he could go, leaving all within the eternal love of God.

God had been preparing him, Allan would say. For years before breaking his neck, Allan had immersed himself in the study of Scripture, developing strong habits of study, reading, and prayer. Over the years, he cultivated

---

1. Eareckson, *Joni*.
2. For a recent discussion about divine providence, see Fergusson, *Providence of God*.

intellectual and theological commitments of the Reformed faith, especially those of the pastor and theologian John Calvin. For Allan, Reformed faith was about living in light of a Christ-shaped reality, responding to that love and being that love to others. And to be open to change.

At its best, as the philosopher Nicholas Wolterstorff has shown, Reformed faith is a holistic view of sin and salvation, shaping vocation and calling. It is the soil for a life shaped by grace, for a journey in and to God as whole persons and for all of creation, for earthly life and the life to come.[3] In recent years, essays and novels by Marilynne Robinson, such as *Gilead*, have captured this spirit beautifully.[4]

From his daily and diligent reading of Scripture to a serious engagement with Calvin's *Institutes of Christian Religion*, which we read together and discussed, and commentaries on the Bible, Allan had formed a strong sense of God's care for his life. This is why even in the moment when the wall broke his neck, a moment of profound loss and life change, Allan saw that God was with him and for him. Rather than being bitter, he wanted to live with gratitude, with love for others. Rather than fall into a life of despair, he lived with hope.

When a few weeks later I was home in Baltimore, I visited Allan in the hospital. "Hey, what's up?" he asked, his head and eyes tilted to the ceiling. Allan had bolts screwed into his skull that held in place a metal "halo" of curved steel that circled around his head. The bolts to the halo steadied his neck in place as the broken neck bones—but not the spinal cord—healed. I'm not sure what I said in response, but I recall that he looked and sounded better than I'd expected. While all of us who visited him in the hospital, and later at the Elizabethtown Rehabilitation center, came to encourage him, Allan worked hard to make us all feel comfortable.

In a reflection that he placed in his journal, Allan described what happened, and how he thought about it:

> *July 5, 1981*
>
> *It's been five weeks and four days since I hit the wall. Although I have never doubted the total sovereignty of God throughout the entire episode, I have often asked him "Why?" This has been by far the hardest time of my life—the excruciating pain at night has been almost unbearable, the realization that I will not be able to do so many things I have loved is tough to deal with—and yet something amazing is true*

---

3. Wolterstorff, *In This World of Wonders*.
4. Robinson, *Death of Adam* and *Gilead*.

> ... I KNOW THAT I AM RICH. *This realization has come about as a direct result of the grace of God, primarily through three channels:*
>
> 1) *Deep times of prayer day and night*
>
> 2) *The body [of Christ] has loved me!*
>
> 3) *Susan has literally been one with me through it all*
>
> *Conclusion: I love God and thank him for the abundance He has given me, and I fully accept His will for my life, in fact with excitement!*

While countless frustrations were an element of daily life for Allan after he hit the wall, as he thought theologically he returned again and again to God's word of care and love as a framing perspective for his life.

In the same year, Allan quoted St. Augustine's response in old age when asked about his health: "In spirit I am well . . . in body I am confined to bed. I can neither walk nor stand nor sit down because of swelling piles . . . Yet even so, since that is the Lord's good pleasure, what should I say but that I am well.'" Able neither to walk nor sit down on his own, Allan yet saw himself as "well" in the Lord.

One evening in 1982, Allan was sitting at his desk, listening to the birds sing outside. "God's creation," Allan wrote by hand, "is beautiful and inviting. Why am I in a chair? I have no idea, but I am beginning to deal with it. Why am I so often oblivious to such obvious grace of God . . . I love and enjoy you, God. Thank you for the song. Thank you for the Light."

But is this take on what he was feeling too easy? Could it be that Allan, despite his profession of trust, of hope in God, was really sublimating anger at God for his injury in ways he never fully or openly acknowledged? Did Allan feel that his injury was somehow merited? Did he seek to justify his suffering and the costs of it to his family with religious language?

Being a person with quadriplegia was a wound at the deepest place of who Allan was in relationship to himself, to God, to Susan, to the girls, and to the world. And after his initial injury, he experienced hospitalization after hospitalization, throughout his life. On countless other occasions, he would be home from the hospital but still need weeks in bed to recover from whatever complication afflicted him because of quadriplegia. Bouts of anger and frustration, felt by Susan first and then those closest to him, were experiences that intensified over time. He kept this space of his life close and did not want others to know about it.

But as far as I can tell, Allan genuinely saw himself as a human being in the presence of a God who directs our steps. Even if he couldn't walk, he could still glorify God with his body. In the language of the Apostles' Creed, Allan believed his life was held by God who is maker of heaven and earth, and in Jesus Christ his Son and our Lord.

In Elizabethtown, or E-town as it was called, the spinal injury rehabilitation center that Allan entered after leaving Shock Trauma, he had to learn all over again to feed and help dress himself, brush his teeth, play with his daughters, and other once simple matters of daily life. After three hard months, expedited because, unsurprisingly, Allan worked overtime, he was fitted for an electric wheelchair and sent home to begin a new life.

While Allan couldn't move the small muscles of his hands, he could curl his fingers and, supplemented with foam grips, could just fit his fingers around a specially devised writing implement that allowed him to type. A finger and palm could also adjust to hold a Flair pen lightly, enabling him to write words at an angle. Because Allan also retained some range of motion in his upper arms, he was able to operate a special set of controls to drive a van. And he could also turn his forearm outward to give his version of a thumbs up.

Susan became Allan's full-time caregiver. It was Susan who stayed with him to deal with and guard against pressure sores, kidney failure, and circulation problems. If Allan had to be somewhere by 9:00 AM, Susan arose at 5:00 AM to tend to him with all his personal and bathroom needs and to help him transfer into his chair, dressed and ready for the day. Then she would care for the girls before getting herself ready.

At the time of Allan's injury, his daughter Jennifer was three years old, and Jessica was nine months old. For the rest of Allan's life, Susan's, Jennifer's, and Jessica's daily routines, vacations, travel, housing, and everything else were deeply affected by Allan's physical needs.

Not long after his injury, Jessica fell into a coma, possibly attributed to viral meningitis, and nearly died. The people who had prayed for Allan's life to be spared when he broke his neck now were doing the same for Jessica. Susan now also cared intensely for Jessica, both in the hospital and throughout convalescence.

A few years later, reviewing the course of his life since breaking his neck, Allan wrote out his thoughts:

> *May 2, 1984*
>
> *A million memories and emotions have just been recalled and relived: the night of the accident in Shock Trauma, having the holes drilled in my head and the tube forced down my throat; seeing Sue*

for the first time there; the utter exhilaration of that; the 5 weeks at the University Hospital with all of the ups and downs, and then the drive to E-town, my first real time out of doors in 5 weeks; the drabness of E-town and the depression of the first day there, with the noise and chaos of the unfriendliness, and the crammed and thoroughly unprivate room; the love and care of so many, especially Sue who I consider more the one with whom I broke my neck and experienced rehab; my parents' constant worry and tears at my situation . . . the sadness and awkwardness of the first Christmas at home to the difficulty of facing a world who still wanted to depend on the old Allan when the new Allan desperately needed time and space. [And yet I was sustained] by the grace of God and a strong understanding of his sovereignty, and even then think how nearly impossible it has been at times to deal with the whole thing. I am both frightened and yet reminded of the fragile state of every man, and realize that joy beyond comprehension awaits me, and a glorified body which will get to spend forever and ever with God in worship.

The book of Job in the Hebrew Bible is about a cry to God when everything seems to go wrong, when the losses are unspeakable. Like Job in the midst of his disruption and loss, Allan was crying out to God.

Allan also prayed for and sought healing. Spinal cord research was beginning to make small strides, and any hint of finding a way to bypass the signals sent by the brain to the body or repair the damage and walk once again drew Allan's attention, his letters and calls inquiring if he was eligible for their trial programs. However, after a few years, his muscles now atrophied and his bones brittle, Allan knew that the possibility of one day walking again in this life had passed.

Yet Allan still spoke of visualizing walking in this life. He also believed and lived as if his broken body, and a world of broken bodies, would experience wholeness, healing, and transformation in the resurrected body of Christ (1 Corinthians 15).[5] The reign of God has come, we read in Mark 1, and "now is the day of salvation," St. Paul announces (2 Corinthians 6:2). In all he did, Allan sought to honor Christ with his life, trusting that God's work was already underway. In his body, in his broken body, he knew the day of salvation.

Our lives are all short, but from the moment Allan hit the wall, he knew that his time was more limited than most. Yet instead of defining his life under the power of death and the reality of his broken body, he defined

---

5. Wright, *Paul and the Faithfulness of God*.

it through his encounter with Jesus who overcame death. Allan lived under the cross and in hope, believing that, in the words of St. Paul written to Roman Christians, "just as Christ was raised from the dead by the glory of the Father, so we too might walk in the newness of life."[6]

This is what I know when Susan calls me to say that after fifty-five years of life on the earth, nearly half these years on the streets of Sandtown, Allan has died.

Through my tears, I walk home, pack a few clothes, collect my pastor's book for funeral services, and take a train to Baltimore to join a community of mourners in Sandtown.

---

6. Romans 6:4.

Prayer

How did Allan say Yes to God's call on his life? How do any of us say Yes to God's call on our lives?

A short time after Allan died, Susan passed along to me two items that spoke to his calling, his fears and his hopes, his desire to follow Christ.

The first was a portrait of Martin Luther King Jr. that had hung in his office over his desk. King inspired Allan not only with a passion for loving God, but also for the nonviolent struggle against poverty, militarism, and racism. King said we should be transformed nonconformists and work to build a beloved community at every level. Allan was all in.[1]

The second item was Allan's set of journals. As a young man, newly married, and still walking, Allan had started keeping a journal, maintaining this practice until a few days before his death. At first the entries are handwritten on the back of scrap paper, but later they are typed, and the pages are organized in recycled binders with names like Gardco Lighting.

Allan's journals, and his journey into vocation and purpose, began with a prayer. His first entry was June 13, 1978:

> *Don't know exactly what lies ahead, but to know that each day spent with you will be an adventure causes me to eagerly anticipate each tomorrow. My main concern, O Lord, is that I would set aside, completely give up, myself and my abilities so totally as to have your work done in your way . . . Father, one thing I know right now is that I long for you to be first in my life. Make me willing to give up anything and everything to serve you.*

---

1. Shelby and Terry, eds., *To Shape a New World*.

Prayer

This prayer became Allan's statement of his life's purpose and calling, his credo, and he returned almost verbatim to it repeatedly across the years of his journal keeping, and more importantly, in his daily life.

Allan's first journal entry, his prayer, reminds me of a prayer found in the Spiritual Exercises of St. Ignatius Loyola:

> Take, Lord,
> and receive all my liberty, my memory,
> my understanding
> and my entire will,
> all that I have and possess.
> You have given all to me to you, Lord, I return it.
> All is yours;
> do with it what you will.
> Give me only your love and your grace,
> that is enough for me.

Although Allan was not familiar with St. Ignatius or the Exercises, these words match his whole-hearted commitment to God.

I think also of a prayer of Charles de Foucauld (1858–1916), who similarly sought a radical commitment to Christ, and who became a hermit who lived and served among the poor before being martyred: "Father," he prayed, "I abandon myself into your hand: do with me what you will." The work that de Foucauld began in the late nineteenth century continues today in cities around the world.

In the years after he wrote such words, Allan breaking his neck would be part of what he understood as "giving up everything." But "offering his life" to God could well mean losing his life, metaphorically certainly, but also literally, by following wherever his love for God and neighbor took him.[2]

Allan's immediate inspiration for his journal keeping was drawn from reading the journals of Jim Elliot, a missionary, a graduate of Wheaton College, a person of unique stature within the evangelical world, a person who chose to shed no blood to protect his life during a mission in South America.[3] Elliott was a more complicated person than Allan saw, but it wasn't the idea of being a missionary that struck Allan, and he never used such language. What most impressed Allan was that Elliott had followed

---

2. Pope Francis, *Maiorem Hac Dilectionem*, on the "offering of life," and Bondi, *To Pray and to Love*.

3. See Saint, "Nate Saint, Jim Elliott, Roger Youderian, Ed McCully and Peter Fleming."

Christ to the fullest possible point, in faith embracing whatever would be, including death. In this he expressed that Elliot was like "a brother" to him, and Allan desired to be like him, a prayer he asked God to grant him.

Journaling was also very tactile for Allan, an act of formation, especially after he broke his neck. For the practice of maintaining a journal was how Allan kept on course with God's purpose for his life, persuading himself over the years that "it was worth it," as he put it.

In *Intimations*, novelist Zadie Smith writes, "Talking to yourself can be useful. And writing means being overheard."[4] For Allan, this was true: journaling was talking to himself, and it was also being overheard—by God. This mode is similar to St. Augustine's *Confessions*, which are a prayer, a dialogue with God.

Allan covered all of daily life in his journals, but there come to be two clear voices, one addressed to God and one to himself to continue work for justice. Much as Gustavo Gutiérrez, in his *On Job: God-Talk and the Suffering of the Innocent*, identifies in Job a contemplative voice of love for God and a prophetic voice for God, a cry for a different world,[5] so too, following his injury and move to Sandtown, these two voices are woven throughout Allan's journaling. A dialogue with God, speaking to himself, and being overheard by God. A dialogue for justice, for growth in grace.

As Allan reflected on God's grace and love for him, even at twenty-three years old and just beginning youth ministry, this act of giving his life completely to the service of God regardless of the cost seemed like the only reasonable thing to do. This was his purpose, and he dedicated himself to this goal. Everything about his life reinforced this.

But it is the life and witness of Dorothy Day that most shaped the course of Allan's life and ministry. After he broke his neck, Allan went back to college, and in 1988, a class assignment was to write one's autobiography. All the expected ground is covered in Allan's: family, upbringing, breaking his neck. But to frame his essay, and to center what he explained he was beginning to do with his family and life in Sandtown, Allan wrote about Day.

Few have understood love in community better, and lived it out more, than Dorothy Day, co-founder with Peter Maurin of the Catholic Worker movement on the Lower East Side of New York City. Day sought to live a faith drawn from the Gospels, especially Matthew 25, which describes Christ as present in the ones who are left out, the mystery of encounter, of

---

4. Smith, *Intimations*, xii.
5. Gutiérrez, *On Job*.

sharing our lives. The Catholic Worker movement started out during the Great Depression with a newspaper that sold for one cent (as it still does today!) and with simple places of hospitality where food and companionship are shared. The movement was a place of living a nonviolent life, of actively living the gospel.

It was not only that Allan now shared Day's pacifism and commitment to the poor that moved him toward her story. Instead, he saw in her life an "idealism" that he wanted to be his, a single-minded focus on something. Allan believed a life marked by a singular passion was "a gift" from God that he had to use, whatever the cost. For Allan, as he found in Robert Coles's portrait of Day, it was not simply her "faith-driven life," but the "drive itself" that resonated with him.[6] Day gave Allan a vision of Christian life that involved commitment and care for others.

Becoming a quadriplegic did not deter Allan from focusing on his vocation. In September 1982, he wrote a prayer in his journal:

> *I have so many times this week wanted to be out of this chair. What a limitation! And Susan put together a photo album of our past couple of years of pictures. Do they ever cause me to desire the normalcy of the olden days, walking and laying around on the floor and swinging the kids around! But it is not to be. God has me here in this place at this time and for His own good reasons. I do believe in its totality in my head, but how hard it is to live this out into the external world. Will I always have to deal with being in the chair with such intensity? Lord please show me it is not a "limitation" because You are sovereign. At any rate, the two thoughts I love regarding this whole situation are that I will be walking with the Father and the saints for all eternity, and [that] the chair keeps me more dependent upon Him in the meantime. And I am determined, by His grace, to carry out all of my desires of work and service regarding the kingdom.*

Allan could only imagine his life as a calling, a service on behalf of God who created and called him, like the psalmist (Psalm 139) and the prophet Jeremiah (Jeremiah 1:5).

This is another point at which the book of Job, which was of immense importance to Allan after he broke his neck, may also reflect back to him his core story before the face of God. It begins with Job as a book about trauma, a cry to God from the depths.[7] As the Franciscan writer Richard

---

6. Coles, *Dorothy Day*.
7. Ford, *Christian Wisdom*, 90–120.

Rohr observed, when Job found himself overwhelmed by trauma, he went even more deeply into this search for an authentic, truthful life.[8] If Job got the chance (so he says), he "would lay [his] case before [God], and fill [his] mouth with arguments. I would learn what [God] would answer me" (23:4–5). But in between making his case and then hearing from God, Job maintained what he believed was right.

In light of Allan's identification with Dorothy Day, I am struck by the memoir her granddaughter, Kate Hennessy, wrote about her: *Dorothy Day: The World Will Be Saved by Beauty, An Intimate Portrait of My Grandmother*.[9] According to her moving account, there were great costs and struggles to Day's idealism and her stubborn love, costs largely borne by her family. The taking of "risks" fell upon her family, and Allan's family, too, and being a quadriplegic had a multiplier effect on the care and life changes required of his family and others.

Calling, vocation, is a gift, but sometimes it can become a curse. If we love God and neighbor, as we see Allan sought so profoundly to do, we are moving forward in a life of faith. But it is fair to say that "calling" can become a "curse" when it makes it hard to listen, to care with gentleness to the needs of others, to hear God. Instead, "calling" can overwhelm. Is there a way of going deeper into the life of God as calling, not simply moving out in action? Can friendship with God break open our categories? Can this reflect the inner direction of our hearts? Whatever the mix of motives and challenges we face, this is part of our humanity.

With his injury, so much had been taken away from Allan. Yet although it had completely changed his life, and connected him to people in their trauma, in other ways becoming a quadriplegic played almost no role in Allan's thinking about ministry. He remained just as focused on vocation as he was before breaking his neck.

This was not possible without Susan, at a great price to her. Throughout his life as quadriplegic, it was Susan who made sure Allan received the ongoing and daily care he needed, interacting with his physicians and clinical care, and managing the problems that arise on the part of patients with complex health conditions. When Sandtown was added, that care almost reached a breaking point. For Allan's calling could become a suffering for others, a life not sought. This is its own journey.

---

8. Rohr, *Job and the Mystery of Suffering*.
9. Hennessy, *Dorothy Day*.

A life worth living, for Allan, was a life of love, service, the giving of his entire self to God and neighbor. This was his preoccupation, witness, and vocation, the center of his humanity, his way of facing death.

Allan also saw his life, with all its possibilities and later infirmities, as praise to God. And he wondered, at the time of his first journal entry, if one day after he had passed, the remembrance of those possibilities and those infirmities might be of encouragement to others.

This was Allan's witness to the character of God, a living and free God who created him, he believed, in love and for love. In response, Allan sought a life dedicated to a passion, at whatever the cost, like an artist.

Describing his own ministry, in Philippians 3:10–14, St. Paul talks of grabbing "hold of that Christ took hold of for me . . . forgetting what lies behind and straining forward to what lies ahead, I press on toward the finish line so that I might win the prize of the heavenly call of God in Christ Jesus."[10] Having been taken hold of by Christ, Allan would grab that which Christ had set before him, to love those things Christ wanted him to love. Allan would not let go, and Christ did not let go of him.

Allan never slowed down in his calling to follow Christ. His heart bare to the face of God, he ran a race of faith. Allan kept saying Yes to Christ's calling in his life.

When the U2 album *No Line on the Horizon* came out in 2009, shortly before he died, Allan listened to the song "Magnificent" many times, struck by the words, "I was born to sing for you . . . from the womb my first cry it was a joyful noise."[11] So clearly did these words express Allan's sense of his life as a calling from God, of a Love from birth that also touched his wounds, that he asked for the song to be included in the liturgy at his funeral. And it was.

---

10. For this translation and important reflections on this text, see Fowl, *Philippians*.
11. U2, "Magnificent."

Signs

Like the lights of a city, signs of God are blinking everywhere. Can we see them? Perhaps even taste them on a warm summer day? All I know is that a Baltimore snowball, a flavored cup of shaved ice sold from a sidewalk stand during the summer months, can be a sign of God, a way that the Spirit will take us forward.

It was the summer of 1986, and Allan and I decided to spend the months driving around the neighborhoods of Baltimore, north, south, east, west, looking for where to move as neighbors. We didn't just put a finger on a map and say "here." Instead, we did our homework. With reams of demographic data, city government reports on housing, and street maps in hand and spread across the back seat of Allan's van, we were seeking not only to identify the neighborhood most overlooked and forgotten in Baltimore, but where we could enter a different story, with God and with a community.

Everything seemed to point to a neighborhood in West Baltimore called Harlem Park. Having spent a good part of a summer day in the Harlem Park neighborhood, we found ourselves at the end of the day at a snowball stand. A Baltimore snowball was just what we needed.

The snowball stand, which consisted of a block of ice, an ice shaver, cups and spoons, and a range of colorful flavors in bottles arrayed on a table, was set up on the sidewalk. I ordered one for Allan and one for me. It was a perfect way to cool down in the humid summer months in Baltimore. I'm sure that if they had it that day my flavor was "Skylite," named for its blue color.

The block with the snowball stand was alive, the windows open, people out on their stoops. Kids were playing games, jumping jacks, maybe Double Dutch, running up and down the block, playing at tag and races combined. There was laughter and joy. I looked up at the street signs: North Mount Street at Laurens. The 1300 block of Mount Street, to be exact.

Signs

Turns out we were actually at a snowball stand in the West Baltimore neighborhood called Sandtown-Winchester, north of and adjacent to Harlem Park. A collection of seventy-two city blocks, it is a community of two- and three-story row homes with a variety of schools, churches, and small businesses; in the near middle of the neighborhood are the 571 dwelling units of the Gilmor Homes public housing community. However, rather than connect seamlessly to the street, they face inward to courtyards, the side walls lining the street, disconnecting the homes from the street and neighborhood.

One day in 1980 when Baltimore's Inner Harbor opened, the *Washington Post* looked two miles west to Sandtown for an extreme contrast. As Ella Johnson, who lived in Sandtown and led the Sandtown-Winchester Improvement Association, told the paper, Sandtown "is just an inner city neighborhood . . . It's buried. A good block is where there are less than five vacant homes."[1]

Bounded by North Avenue and Lafayette to the north and south, and Monroe and Pennsylvania Avenue with a bit of Freemont to the west and east, the neighborhood is two miles west of the Inner Harbor, a mile or so more to Mondawmin Mall. Sandtown-Winchester was likely named for the sand that at one time spilled out from the horse drawn carts traveling through the neighborhood from a nearby quarry, and Winchester was a street named for George Winchester, whom reports indicate was a nineteenth-century president of the Baltimore and Susquehanna Railroad, and was also involved in city planning and building up the port.[2] Most people just called the neighborhood Sandtown.

How did we come this point of moving to Sandtown? That snowball stand moment in Sandtown takes me back to five years earlier when Allan and Susan came to visit me at college. That year I was living off-campus in a house trailer. It was their first real time away since Allan had hit the wall and finished physical rehab. I located and put in place a plywood board to serve as a ramp for Allan's chair to roll up the small set of steps and into the trailer. And whatever Susan would claim in later years, I had prepared a feast for them of fish sticks for famished travelers. Only it was frozen solid and needed to be cooked. We spent the next few days visiting New City Fellowship and talking about our faith, lives, future, and my dubious culinary skills.

1. Saperstein, "Sandtown Typical of Urban Blight."
2. Ryon, *West Baltimore Neighborhoods*, 124; Rauch, "George Winchester."

Sharing the Crust

When they got back home, Allan wrote to me, addressing me with a nickname he had coined a year earlier on our trip to the Boundary Waters in Canada:

> *August 28, 1982*
>
> *Reverend Graynik—*
>
> *Mark, it's been definitely a blessing to me to spend time with you the past couple of months. I have really appreciated your love towards me, from last summer with visits to Etown all the way to the present time . . .*
>
> *The question is, how can we truly affect the world in a truly radical sense? I know you desire this as much as I do; we need to continue both thinking and dialoguing until it all computes into action . . .*
>
> *I really look forward to whatever lies ahead. It may be that some of us work closely together; that would be nice, but God is indeed sovereign.*
>
> *I'll see you in a couple of weeks, unless some maniac pushes the wrong button.*
>
> *Allan*

Here, with just a few words, Allan writes with conviction, a sense of humor, and an allusion to the immorality and madness of nuclear weapons, but he also conveys that he saw in me a calling, a "Rev," a vocation to serve Christ, and I think implied something of the same in himself, and us together. Perhaps with others we could "affect the world in a truly radical sense."

Now, as we were driving around Baltimore together, Allan and Susan had a wheelchair-accessible home in rural Clarksville, Maryland, where they continued together in youth ministry. I was living in West Philadelphia and completing seminary. But Allan had been growing increasingly restless, wanting to do more with his life, a movement in his spiritual journey, his itinerary of faith.

By the winter of 1985, Allan wrote as much in his journal:

> *I am ready to relocate in the city and minister to the community in which I live! I sense great calling without the actual needs or my role. The idea of being effective there in the chair is overwhelming almost to the point of despair, but I can't let this deter me if it is calling, which it strongly is.*

As Allan reflected in his journal the same year, "The question is no longer whether God is on the side of the poor and oppressed, but where should I locate to be involved with them?"

Now that I was completing theological studies, Allan and I began to meet weekly, usually "half way" at a rest stop on I-95 between Baltimore and Philadelphia. Finding a table, at the Chesapeake House rest stop along I-95, mixed in with late-night truck drivers and travelers around us, over endless cups of coffee for Allan and tea for me, we talked until the early morning hours. We discussed our faith, Scripture, family, his life as a quad, politics, and film. And of course, especially music, like the Irish band U2 and the Canadian musician and songwriter Bruce Cockburn, who both connected Christian spirituality with the political and social times. U2's *Unforgettable Fire* and Cockburn's *Stealing Fire* were albums that spoke to our faith.

Through listening to music and conversation, Allan and I grew in insight, in understanding, in friendship, in the Word. And we laughed about Allan's definition of "half way," as I always ended up with the longer drive.

But whatever we talked about, we would always come back to doing something together in Baltimore, nearly an examination of conscience. How could we use the gifts God had given us for the peace and healing of our world? How could we live a life of faith and repentance in the face of historic racism? What would it mean for us to take up John Perkins's challenge to live in and not just visit a community, to be of best use as neighbors?

At that time, entire neighborhoods across America were being abandoned and left in ruins, histories and communities discarded and thrown away as if unimportant. The photographer Camilo José Vergara, going from city to city—New York, Newark, Detroit, Gary, and Baltimore among them—documented what was taking place right before our eyes: photographs of urban remains, their afterlives, and continued struggles.[3] Like we find in the book of Lamentations, cities are crying out in distress, offering a lament to God. There is a search for healing.

As we considered these signs of the times, the inner story of our conversations was around the meaning of memory, sin, and salvation. Because history, the essayist Cathy Park Hong reminds us, has a moral hold on us, then how, Allan and I asked, should *we* rightly remember the past, *our past*

---

3. Vergara, *American Ruins,* and *Detroit is No Dry Bones.*

and its role in the life and world we inhabited, a world where so much in our city and nation had been built by racial injustice and social division?[4]

After college, I had returned to Mississippi and for a year became a part of Voice of Calvary. Living in Harambee House, I learned from my roommates about poverty in the Delta and life after Parchman Prison. I grew just by being around people like Lem Tucker, Donna and Chris Rice, and the Perkins family. At Voice of Calvary, I was able to see up close not only how important its ministry is, from addressing poverty and racism in the city to helping with life after prison, but also how difficult such ministry and church life can be. Rather than discourage me, this made me aware early on of many potential pitfalls, struggles, and often ambiguities that go along with this kind of work.

Allan and I felt called to take on John Perkins's three Rs of *relocation* as the commitment to a place, *reconciliation* as the larger story of what God is doing in the world, and *redistribution* as the economics of God's kingdom in Baltimore. We added a fourth R, *repentance*, to recognize and turn from sin as something rooted in the past, in our story.

The idea of repentance is *metanonia*, a change of direction, a conversion, turning our lives in a new direction so that we might think, work, and live differently, as St. Paul wrote in Romans 12:1–2. Given the history and systems of racism, we felt called to work for justice, to move in a different way. Repentance is a foundation for building communion with God, our neighbors, and all of creation, bringing freedom and joy. This commitment, a choice of loyalty to Jesus as Savior and Lord, would challenge us and change our lives.

Not long after that day on which we enjoyed snowballs on North Mount Street, after we learned more, talked, and prayed, Allan reached out to and met with Ella Johnson, who led—really *was*—the Sandtown-Winchester Improvement Association, the local neighborhood organization. After explaining the reasons that we were praying about moving to Sandtown, Ella offered her blessing. I'm sure she thought we were crazy, but she gave us a chance. Thank you, Ella.

What were we thinking? Susan was being realistic, honest, and clear-minded about the change to their lives. She thought Allan and I didn't have any idea what we were doing, although to be fair she'd also thought this before Sandtown. Now, Susan observed, Allan's passion to move to Sandtown, his desire and clarity, and my support, had run ahead of considering

---

4. Hong, *Minor Feelings*.

its implications for his medical care, for the extra work all of this placed upon Susan and the family.

After more than a year of planning, we put our plans for Sandtown on hold. I began to think about what to do if I were no longer moving back to Baltimore.

Sometimes such significant decisions need time. After some months of reconsideration, and near despair by Allan, we decided to move ahead. Susan did so out of her own inner sense of call, her choice to commit her life to being a neighbor, even if she was angry with Allan for the way he was proceeding. Over time, her call would deepen and expand, and years later, whatever changes would come, Susan would still live in Sandtown, as part of a community.

But Susan was right: the move and the attendant life changes fell upon her more than Allan. If it was messy, Allan couldn't think of another way, but his inability to do so was quintessential Allan.

In one way, "relocating" would be a small act, some would even say a personal or individual calling. It was how we took responsibility, deciding to enter into the struggle for life in Sandtown. But given the segregation dynamics of Baltimore, evidenced in highways, housing, schools, stores, and church life, it was much more than that, for it was a challenge to the underlying systems of exclusion, and choices we often make to avoid involvement. We never get everything fully right, but with the insights and grace we could prayerfully discern at that moment, we believed that a responsible action for us was to "relocate" to Sandtown as neighbors. To join in what God was already doing in Sandtown.

Writing in his journal Allan considered what this moment of change would mean for him:

> *May 7, 1987*
>
> *I keep thinking, "I don't need to do this. I'm uprooting my wife and kids, a lot of which has been hell already, and thinking of what they will now miss out on that I had as a kid, and thinking how easy it would be to remain here where it is at least placid." But I know what has to happen, and I know that it will not be easy. It is where history is and where we need to be at any and all cost—I think. I do know I love God and wholly desire to do whatever he wants me to, convinced that it is Sandtown beyond any shadow of a doubt.*

For Allan, family existed for love of neighbor and the kingdom of God. That's why, if anything, Allan wished he and Susan, Jenny, and Jessica, had moved "ten years" earlier.

By the time Allan wrote this, I had already moved to Sandtown at the end of the previous year, renting a house at 1125 North Calhoun Street, as I commuted back and forth to Philadelphia, where I soon completed seminary.

One morning, I looked up and saw a neighbor from across the street, leaning out his window telling me his name and asking me mine, *My name is Frank! What's your name?* Frank Ross was the first person I met, or rather it was Frank who met me on Calhoun Street. From that day forward, Frank would be close to everything in our shared story, and in friendship with Kelly Simpkins, who was there at the beginning.

A year later, I moved from Calhoun Street to 1304 North Mount Street, where I took off the weather-faded plywood covering the doorways, put in windows, added plumbing and a new roof, and fixed the stairs. Enough just to move in!

My new neighbor was Ike, and we became lifelong friends.

But amazingly, this was the block on Mount Street with the snowball stand where Allan and I had first stopped in the neighborhood. Maybe even the very house outside of which we'd stopped!

What God was opening us to in Sandtown was God's community of love and friendship. Rather than begin with a vision of what could be in our context, we would find our way step by step, together with others by being in a place. We were on a journey to new creation.[5] Together, we were finding out how God was present in all things.

Turns out a Baltimore snowball on a muggy humid summer day really can be a holy sign of God's purposes for the world, for a journey and a future. Maybe this is why when summer comes around, I can't wait to have a Baltimore snowball!

---

5. Katongole, *Journey of Reconciliation*.

Chess

"Our life and our death is with our neighbor," Anthony the Great observed many years ago. In Sandtown, our life together, and love of neighbor, was found in a game of chess on stoop.

It was the summer of 1987, and Allan, Susan, Jennifer, and Jessica, "daughters nine and six," were now living on the 1000 block of North Gilmor Street. Allan slept on a cot set up in the front room, next to the table where they took their meals; to get into the house, he came in through an alley filled with trash and rats.

Weasel, with his new neighbor Allan, played many games on the Gilmor Street stoop. Over pawns, kings, queens, and rooks moving around the board, they began to hear one another's stories. They talked about their families, their backgrounds, their health, and their favorite chess moves. But even for Weasel, I doubt that Allan put aside his competitive spirit.

Meanwhile Allan, Susan, and family learned firsthand about housing conditions in Sandtown so bad I'm still at a loss for words to describe them. From rotting floors to doors that didn't close properly and thin walls painted and painted over, electrical systems that could run only a few lightbulbs operated by pull strings, to infestations of rodents in what passed for a kitchen, the houses surely should not have passed a housing or health inspection. But this was the condition everywhere in the neighborhood.

Each block in Sandtown is a little part of the city, a world of families, extended families with grandparents, cousins, uncles and aunts, and networks of friends. The sidewalks are places of laughter, fussing, running, playing, hanging out, going to the basketball court, or just meeting friends. Relationships are the connective tissue in the neighborhood, running across the streets and blocks, corner stores, and neighbors. This is how we learned about the local schools, religious life, the recreation center. About daily life, where nothing is settled, so each day people had to find their way, to make things work.

In Allan's first years in Sandtown, he also became friends with Pull, Elwood, and others on the Gilmor block. Then there was Damon, who introduced Allan to his mother Linda and her sister LaVerne, and also Louise. Damon was both serious and gracious, and he and Allan grew to care deeply for one another. And also for the family, Lisa, Patrice, and Garrie. As a family, they had a deep connection and memories of the neighborhood, a care for the good of all, and a faith that was tough. And for Thomas from up the block, too.

Gary and his brother Hamp and mother Darlene became friends with Allan, Susan, Jenny and Jessica. Gary was shy and loved starting new things. Allan also grew close to Fitt Bennett and his mother Erlene. Fitt was young, with a great sense of humor, and knew everybody, a bridge between Allan and the community.

Fitt and Gary adopted the Tibbels and became extended family. Man and Toy also became close with the Tibbels. We met Torrey and her family, and Lucky, also known as Bubby, who very much became a person whom Allan loved. His family was also in Sandtown. Frank was around for everything we did, with an easy way of making new friends. He lived on North Calhoun with his mother Hilda and his younger brother Rodney.

As neighbors on North Mount Street, Ike and I became friends on the MacAbees basketball courts, which are part of the Gilmor Homes. Ike, I could see right away, was a leader, compassionate and caring for everyone around him. After the heat of the summer sun waned in the evening, I would go over to the basketball court and join in any games that were underway. Not only did I play basketball with Ike, and make a few shots now and then, I also met his friends, including Arteze, Luck, Big Man, Jermaine, and Anton. And then Miss Joanne, Miss Holly, Miss Carol. And it wasn't long before I reconnected with Kurt, whom I had met many years earlier.

Renay Kelley was a highly respected adult and friend to almost every kid and family in Sandtown and was known everywhere in the neighborhood simply as Mr. Kelley. A pastor by calling, Mr. Kelley was the leader of the Lillian P. Jones Recreation Center at the time. He was always there as a trusted adult and leader in the neighborhood, caring for the kids, no matter his actual job title. Allan first got to know Mr. Kelley when he volunteered at the "Rec Center."

In Sandtown, we are all very conscious of the differences of race, class, and history; it is in the air we breathe, the reality of our city, our stories. Sandtown was more than 99 percent black, and Allan, Susan, and I were white. Allan, Susan, and I knew the judgment, and the grace of God, in our stories. We knew things could have gone differently. Around the same time that we moved to Sandtown, an African American family moved into an all-white neighborhood in Baltimore, only to be harassed and forced out.

When we were asked why we moved to Sandtown, our answer was simple: "to be neighbors."

We learned a theology of being a neighbor.[1] As we read Scripture, we became deeply aware that loving one's neighbor is a summary of biblical faith, the other side of loving God. Interpersonal yes, but also profoundly social. Throughout Scripture, to be a neighbor entails creating a web of relationships marked by honor, dignity, significance, responsibility, and justice. For the Hebrew prophets, being a neighbor is not just about being concerned, it is about responding to oppression and injustice.

To be a neighbor is to share life. And to share life is to be human; it is to be attentive to the basics of food, shelter, family, dreams, the basketball court, struggles, and complexities. It is to be a neighbor to the neighborhood, to all of creation, to all of God's world.

As neighbors, the most basic thing we can do is bring our stories to one another, to open ourselves to life as we each see and experience it. A good word for this is *accompaniment*, sharing life together and becoming friends along the way. It is essential, as the Peruvian priest Fr. Gustavo Gutiérrez states, to be present, to listen, to pray, to be alongside one another, sharing our joys, burdens, and difficulties over time. This is solidarity, being a neighbor to one another.[2] It is the simplicity not of doing but of being. Of staying in a place, staying with one another.

Allan's way of being in the neighborhood was to see each person as called by God, then support their vocation, working it out in countless small ways of encouragement, commitment, and solidarity. This was as he had done for years before in youth ministry. In a few words, it is about friendship over the long haul.

---

1. Gutiérrez, *Theology of Liberation*, 202–3. As he writes, "A theology of the neighbor . . . has yet to be worked out" (203). On neighbors and friends, see O'Donovan, *Entering into Rest*, 135–38.

2. Gutiérrez, *Theology of Liberation*, 202–3. For further reflection, see Farmer and Gutiérrez, *In the Company of the Poor*, and Gutiérrez, *Spiritual Writings*.

Sharing the Crust

Trust is the gift that makes such a life together in friendship possible. Trust is also at the core of Christian thought and practice. In Christian faith, God trusts us, granting us the gift of our choices, the way we build and sustain our relationships. Trust is also a social practice; it is the way communities and relationships are held together. And trust is also belief, trusting in God. In other words, trust from God, in God, and with one another is critical to life and community.[3] It is what we were given by God in and for one another.

Because of his brokenness as a quadriplegic, and because he embodied the impact of trauma, people with their own wounds trusted Allan, spoke with him, shared with him. Each of us as a person not only suffers, but also suffers differently, but Allan was closest to those who suffered from addictions, the loss of family members, the lack of health care alongside many ailments, and the scarcity of resources. It was for Allan an "attitude" toward one's own infirmities and the needs of others, something that had to be "developed" over time, he found.[4]

The New Testament often talks about the Christian life as taking place through the body, and in fact a broken body. As St. Paul says,

> We always carry around in our body the death of Jesus, so that the life of Jesus may also be revealed in our body. For we who are alive are always being given over to death for Jesus' sake, so that his life may also be revealed in our mortal body. So then, death is at work in us, but life is at work in you. (2 Corinthians 4:10–12)

Allan's body, with all that came with the damage to his spinal cord, was also forming his way of thinking and living.[5] Whatever Allan was unable to feel physically, he was never numb or detached to the world and people around him. He carried Christ's life around in all of who he was, as if in "jars of clay" (2 Corinthians 4:7), just like so many in Sandtown.[6]

This dimension of what it meant to be human, the lens of sharing our physical vulnerability, was how the Carmelite Saint Thérèse of Lisieux came to mean so much to Allan. His journey alongside her story began one Sunday when we went to Washington to view *Thérèse*, Alain Cavalier's 1987 cinematic portrait of the saint. For Allan, it wasn't just a film.

---

3. See Morgan, *Roman Faith*.

4. For one view of how these themes are the heart of spirituality in Scripture and history, see Young, *Brokenness and Blessing*.

5. On bodies as thinking, see Engelke, *How to Think*, 160.

6. See Young and Ford, *Meaning and Truth*.

Seeing *Thérèse* both expressed and helped to shape Allan's desires, the "core of his being" as he put it. What was so compelling to Allan about Thérèse, as he wrote in his journal, was her "singleness of purpose and unswerving commitment to carry out her desire to love Christ at any cost are a lesson. All of life—literally every second, every minute [and] action—are to be lived with the realization of their significance and in relationship with Christ."

The image from the film that was most impactful upon Allan was one of sacrifice. At the bedside of a fellow sister, Thérèse knowingly took on her tuberculosis. As Allan recorded in his journal, this pattern of self-giving, of "suffering" with, as Thérèse exhibited it, was "not only [to be] accepted, but desired" for his life.

That Thérèse of Lisieux is known as the patron saint of Christian mission is a connection that Allan did not make but is likely more important than we realized for our common experience of witness in Sandtown. Her path of "the little way," attentiveness to people and God through the small things that express love, care, and solidarity, was Allan's way of proceeding in Sandtown.

As we lived only a few blocks apart, Allan and I met at least once a day to talk and pray together, most days over lunch, often hot dogs, and a milk from a nearby 7-Eleven. In our own form of an examen, each day we asked how God was inviting us into a greater passion for God, and to more and more love as God loves Sandtown.

We wanted to see, following St. Ignatius, how God was in everything in Sandtown. To this end, we sought to see each person, building, corner store, dog and cat, basketball court, water pipe, empty lot, and street the way God looks at it. Our spiritual strength was being drawn from one another in Sandtown, from the neighborhood. The goal was to have the ears and the eyes, even the skin, attuned to God being experienced through the neighborhood.

It was an immersion of the senses. We were listening, learning, having our eyes opened, allowing space for the Spirit to work on our hearts, being present in gratitude for life in the neighborhood. It was a way of praying as we went. And as Allan would say to his neighbors then and for the remainder of his years, "Thank you for letting me be here."

But mostly, we thought, our presence was comic relief for the neighborhood! Allan as a quad in an electric wheelchair and, I as a young guy, with longish hair and round wire-rimmed glasses, up and about in

Sandtown at all hours of the night and day. At least, Allan said, we made some kind of contribution! How could we ever take ourselves too seriously?

At the invitation of Ella Johnson, Allan and I become active participants in the Sandtown-Winchester Improvement Association. The more we got to know Ella Johnson, the more we were moved by her leadership in the neighborhood, deploying the limited public resources available to her with tact and skill to serve people in Sandtown. After a while, she invited us to become board members.

Ella put us to work! We regularly walked—or, in Allan's case, rode—every single block and alley street in the neighborhood, going from door to door, delivering mimeographed legal-paper–sized flyers announcing community meetings and other relevant information about neighborhood programs. Ike, Anton, Jenny, Jessica, and others all joined the work.

We came to understand that each block was its own world, complete with a fire hydrant for summer cooling and the watchful eyes of neighbors throughout the year. We learned about the neighborhood through its different streets, main ones like Carey, and interior alley streets like Parrish that held just a few remaining houses. And we learned more about our neighbors, and they learned about us.

For Allan, being present mattered most. "Simply living here with our neighbors," Allan wrote in his journal, "is in many ways enough for me."

But because of God's love for Sandtown, as Allan considered the conditions—the fires, the slow-moving mass shooting events, the menacing sounds of the police foxtrot helicopter, the lack of grocery stores, substandard housing—he became angry. At one point, recalling the face of one of the young people in the neighborhood, he thought of her "lack of options" and he cried. "The tears were both of a deep sadness and a rage because it is so unfair."

Lament was an important word and theme for us in Sandtown. As the priest and theologian Emmanuel Katongole shows, lament does not mean to turn inward, to give up, but instead to look outward into a world that cries out for healing.[7] This prayer, a lament, was the source of Allan's passionate commitment to justice, to the well-being of Sandtown as a neighbor. To lament, to suffer with, is a cry to God for justice, as we find in the book of Joel and the Psalms, in the death of Christ on the cross. I think that here, with lament, is where Allan's solidarity and sensitivity to injustice in the neighborhood, shaped him.

---

7. Katongole, *Born from Lament*.

Chess

Two years after moving into a tiny rental house on North Gilmor Street, Allan and Susan purchased and renovated two side-by-side dilapidated houses on North Stricker Street, wide enough for a wheelchair ramp, and moved in, carrying with them the rhythms of Gilmor Street. Here, in some of Allan's journal reflections, we find two characteristics of his ministry—relationality and planning for the next day:

> *July 22, 1988*
>
> *Took Fitt to Mount Clare today for bike parts . . . Frank started a job on Wednesday . . . Mark and I visited Fort McHenry a week ago to check it out for a picnic. We then went to check out seating for me at Memorial Stadium. It was a blast [watching the Orioles] . . . I'll be taking kids to a game soon . . . Hung with neighbors quite a bit: Davises, Rita, Thomas a little, and I met Charles on the stoop. Oh, and Rosalyn, whose birthday is tomorrow so that I need to get a card by then.*

His day was a hectic reality, but this was life in the neighborhood. Rosalynn and family, and the Davis family, neighbors on both sides of his home, became friends with Allan, Susan, and family. In thoughts written down in his journal late at night on July 25, 1988, Allan reflected:

> *I am—I am exhausted. I can hear a few people and a radio at the Davises . . . Charlene has become a very good friend; they all have. I love living on this block . . . Basically, my days the past few weeks have consisted of hanging with people in the neighborhood. Jen and Jess play with Nita, Tyra and Shaconda, who are in our house every day. Jen got skates (at Toys R Us with Tyra and Shaconda) and Jess is using Jenny's old ones, so skating has been the main event the past few days . . . There are a million other things . . . but I'm going to bed.*

From a collage of stories, leaders, families, and histories, games of chess, God was creating among us a new story and community! As neighbors, we found a daily life together of the mundane, the joyful, moments of play and laughter, times of hope, loss, prayer, disappointment, and tears. In the neighborhood, we learned solidarity, respect, mutuality.

Those first years also taught us something about social change: it rarely begins in promising ways. Among those of us who moved to Sandtown, we faced our own misunderstandings, disagreements, and disappointments. We faced personal losses. All of this was painful, and sometimes relationships became broken.

But change, we found in Sandtown, begins at the personal level with our own stories, and in our stories in face-to-face encounters, in relationships. Such friendship is slow work, and there is no shortcut. But one plus one in relationships leads to more than the sum of its parts: it leads to more relationships, and then to the work of building and strengthening a common life, institutions, and then, we also pray, to change in wider society. To honoring the claims of justice and grace. This pattern is not unique; it is the story found in the Gospels.

Beginning with our stories is what the book of Ruth is about, and it mirrored our experience. The story of Ruth in the Hebrew Scriptures is an account of two women, Naomi and Ruth, who despite differences in age and background each took on the risk and unknowns of relationship. In the journey of life and difference, they came to a place of redemptive trust and shared strength. Ruth and Naomi, out of their loss, took a journey together to something new and vital. They formed a small community of belonging on the move, arriving at a place of companionship with God and one another.[8] Crossing boundaries, taking risks, each person is subject to costs, criticism, and misunderstanding. But ultimately, that is how they, and we, can find the life God offers to us.

In Sandtown, we found our life and death with our neighbors. We found unexpected friendships, deepening who we were in God, and bringing us closer to God.[9] We found friendship as a sacrament of vulnerability and of humanity. It is such vulnerable friendship, and love in community, in a particular place and time, that is the heart of our story and our new identity in Christ.

Our life and death with one another, the ongoing transformation of our lives, in and for Sandtown, this was our founding story given by Christ. Our *charism*. Making real our new relationship in the Word. Beginning with games of chess on the stoop!

---

8. Florer-Bixler, *Fire by Night*, 169–81.

9. Radcliffe, "Shaped by Tenderness, the Most Beautiful Thing on Earth."

Furniture

What is it like to have every single one of your family's possessions—your children's clothes, your only couch, family photographs, birth certificates, books, and kitchen chairs—piled up on the curb in front of your home? The possibility of being "put out"— the neighborhood term for being evicted—was seemingly a possibility for everyone in Sandtown.

One winter morning in 1987, when I was still living on Calhoun Street, I noticed a person moving quickly up and down the block, delivering something through what seemed like every house's mail slot. They weren't advertising flyers; they were eviction notices. And as Frank, who lived across the street, explained, this happened regularly.

Being put out can shatter a sense of self and place for children and parents, for families across generations.[1] But it's not just furniture and other possessions that end up on the street, it's also the dreams and hopes that a family has.

On top of this, the houses in Sandtown were toxic—literally poisonous—as they were often filled with lead paint. For years after living on Calhoun Street I received letters from Baltimore law firms inquiring whether I would like them to represent me in a lawsuit against my former landlord for lead poisoning. One of the deadliest results of lead poisoning, even a small amount, is the damage it does to the development of a child's brain, which then can affect learning, and in turn job prospects, family life, and much more.

With the courts functioning almost as a predatory collection agency, at little cost to landlords, and with little legal recourse and time or resources to work things out when you are on the edge of being put out, or just now

---

1. For some broader further reflections, see Bouma-Prediger and Walsh, *Beyond Homelessness*, and Holton, *Longing for Home*.

on the street, eviction, as the sociologist Matthew Desmond shows in his study *Evicted*, catches you in a cycle of almost never being able to get ahead economically, thereby keeping families in poverty.[2]

When we asked people, we found that the amount owed was typically a mere few hundred dollars or less. As we wrote up in one of our first church newsletters, a study at the time by the Baltimore City Court showed that 80,072 eviction notices were filed in 1987, resulting in over 5,072 evictions across the city. This meant that Sandtown, and Baltimore, had one of the highest rates of evictions in the nation.

Whenever we learned that an eviction was about to take place in the neighborhood, as quickly as we could, Allan, Ike, Fitt, Gary, and I, and many others, would make our way to the house in question. Each time, we offered to pay the rent that was due to the people involved in the eviction, or just hand over all we had as a start, trying to reason for more time. As best as I can recall, we never stopped a single eviction, at least for more than a few days.

At the request of Ella Johnson, I visited families in Sandtown facing disputes with their landlords. We would walk though their house, writing down the problems, which was really everything, from the kitchen to the wiring to plumbing to doors, and then I would type them up. You could see the landlord was charging high rent, making no repairs or any regular upkeep, then evicting, and beginning all over again. I never heard of a successful challenge by a tenant.

Baltimore, Sandtown, faces not just an eviction and housing crisis, but a crisis of belonging, which is moral and spiritual. How can we even begin to see this world differently without the bonds of love, formed by the moral, and spiritual, and political commitments we must have for one another? How do we recognize the cries we do not hear or heed, the people we do not see? How do we consider the crucified Christ in this place, as Jürgen Moltmann challenges us?[3]

What seemed then and now most profoundly missing was an imagination for the common good, a different way of seeing, thinking, and feeling about the city. What was absent was a politics of belonging in place of indifference, a commitment to biblical justice instead of abandonment and exclusion. And with this, that there can be dignity and justice for families in our neighborhoods.

2. Desmond, *Evicted*.
3. Moltmann, *Crucified God*.

Only in later years when I visited the South African cities of Johannesburg and Cape Town, with their legacies of apartheid then still deeply etched into the urban fabric of high rise downtowns, increasingly forlorn and abandoned, and informal housing that stretched for miles, would I physically feel lines and conditions of race, space, and opportunities drawn as sharply as they were in Baltimore.

As in so many American cities, so too in South African cities you can see and feel the divisions, two cities in one, one Black, one white. It is these patterns and structures, highways built and stopped, bus routes, stores, and schools, that affect families and neighborhoods every day, impacting life outcomes for good or harm.[4]

You can literally see these two-in-one cities. The public and community health scholar Lawrence Brown, in *The Black Butterfly*, describes how the geography of Baltimore is shaped. Black Baltimore looks a "butterfly," with East and West Baltimore joined together, while white Baltimore looks like an "L," from the Inner Harbor to the Guilford neighborhoods. This is the reality of the geographical pattern of hyper urban segregation, rooted in laws, history, and policies that shape everything about life and its outcomes in the city.[5]

Race is central to the story of Baltimore because racial segregation is at the center of the city's history, politics, and geography. The "ghosts" of slavery and racism in history, institutions, and economic life haunt Maryland and Baltimore. For more than one hundred years long, as the *Baltimore Sun* reporter Antero Pietila recounts in *Not in My Neighborhood: How Bigotry Shaped a Great American City*,[6] laws and legal covenants were enshrined in Baltimore city law. As Pietilla shows, this is still keeping people apart, privileging white families and merchants over Black ones.

These laws determined not only where people lived, but where banks invested money, where public funds were allocated, and how the city developed. As Lawrence Brown shows, this affects health and well-being in systemic ways.

In segregated Baltimore, Sandtown was originally developed as a white community, with change arriving as the African American population and institutions moved from east to west in the city. Sharon Baptist Church would create a home on Stricker Street, St. Peter Claver on

---

4. For a full analysis, see Brown, *Black Butterfly*.
5. Brown, *Black Butterfly*.
6. See Pietila, *Not in My Neighborhood*. See also Rothstein, *Color of Law*.

Freemont Ave. By the Second World War, Sandtown was an African American neighborhood.[7]

After the Second World War, Sandtown's population reached some thirty-five thousand residents, filling every house, school, and street. Some small- and medium-sized factories could now be found in the neighborhood, a Schmidt's bakery and Capitol Cake Company among them. On Pennsylvania Avenue, shops, places to eat, and small businesses thrived along with jazz clubs and theaters. The Gilmor Homes were built in 1941 for defense workers.

By the 1980s, jobs were disappearing, as the esteemed Harvard sociologist William Julius Wilson observed.[8] As part of that wave, manufacturing jobs like those at the Sparrows Point steel mill disappeared, with little to take the place of the wages and benefits it offered, affecting west Baltimore neighborhoods like Sandtown. Capital moved elsewhere, even as the most vulnerable could not. Resources and attention went elsewhere, including to one war after another, not least to the "war on drugs." As Willa Bickham and Brendan Walsh of Viva House in South Baltimore put it, "the poor got sent away empty."[9]

Almost anywhere on the streets of Sandtown, you could see the physical collapse of buildings and infrastructure, the effects of a history of systemic disinvestment and abandonment, of a different type of war. Beirut, Lebanon was the city to which we most often first compared Sandtown, Beirut being a city where a war claimed countless lives, displaced much of the population, and turned much of the city to rubble.

Statistics don't easily tell the stories of lives lived, but they can help us see social realities. Families got by—or didn't—on around $7,000 a year, according to 1980 statistics. The official unemployment rate of 22 percent was comparable to that of the Great Depression, but the real number was almost certainly twice as high.[10] As data then and now shows, children and young people particularly faced major obstacles to growing up in health and well-being.[11]

---

7. Ryon, *West Baltimore Neighborhoods*, 126–29.

8. Wilson, *When Work Disappears*.

9. Walsh and Bickham, *Long Loneliness in Baltimore*.

10. The statistics are from the Baltimore Department of Housing and Community Development Planning Division, the 1980 US Census, and other sources.

11. For one study, see DeLuca et al., *Coming of Age*.

FURNITURE

The number of vacant houses on every block reflected a population declining dramatically. In 1980, just 12,248 people lived in the neighborhood.

With highways built to connect people to the suburbs, away from the city, subsidizing not only the move but cars and land to support it, neighborhoods became disconnected and segregated. Scant and unreliable public transportation compounded the problem, and with few job prospects and jobs with wages capable of supporting a family, for most people cars and their insurance were literally out of reach. No wonder that many street corners became drug markets, drugs being a certain source of employment. No wonder that in 1980, the public health data for Sandtown—including infant mortality, adult morbidity rates, and gun violence—were among the most disheartening in the city. For too many, living in Sandtown meant death before their time.

Sandtown is in the Western District, and the location of the Western Baltimore Police Department headquarters was on North Mount Street. The atmosphere was one of patrol cars racing around the streets, unmarked and undercover knocker teams of police stopping young men on their way to school or work, the store, or a friend's, making them drop their pants to be searched right there on the street. And Foxtrot, the police helicopter, contributed to that atmosphere, with its constant heavy hovering, especially at night. The whole experience was like living under occupation, as in a war zone.

If the challenge facing Sandtown was and is systemic, the burdens were and are personal. Parents, families, often must make choices about paying either the rent, utilities, or groceries. Young people knew few who went on to high school, and even fewer who graduated. Trauma was embedded in daily life, from seeing the impact of gun violence from an early age, and other forms of violence, and it touched every family.

The writer Ta-Nehisi Coates, who grew up in West Baltimore,[12] wrote a book framed as a letter to his son, titled *Between the World and Me*, that includes descriptions of his experience of growing up in Baltimore. In it, Coates recounts a continual struggle to survive against forces that threatened him—and still threaten Black bodies. In many parts of Baltimore, he writes, the fear of death can "billow up like fog."[13]

Not for a minute would conditions in Sandtown be deemed acceptable to the wider public and the authorities if it were Ruxton, a white and

---

12. Coates, *Beautiful Struggle*.
13. Coates, *Between the World and Me*, 20.

affluent neighborhood less than twenty minutes away, where I grew up. As new neighbors in Sandtown, Allan, Susan, and I could see as never before the scandal of a whole society allowing neighborhoods like Sandtown to exist in their abandonment, and wonder how people could keep up the struggle for life.

The reality of Sandtown was our context, and the conditions were not only difficult, and surreal, especially when compared to other neighborhoods, but they were also an affront to God, to the image of God in each person. Such conditions are sinful as they break the bond of God's friendship with creation, with the most vulnerable.[14]

Journaling just a few days after moving to Sandtown, Allan analyzed this reality:

> Striking to me after having hung in the neighborhood for a couple of days was a fact which I had always "known" but not really: the neighborhood was all Black and poor. I remember when this realization struck me, and I thought, "How did this come to be? How in the hell did things turn out like this?" And of course the questions are rhetorical. Sadly, we know why things are this way.

The "obvious" answer for Allan was found in history, and the development of the city and nation.

There is a theological element too. William Stringfellow thought about the deep structure of sin and the power of death in society. Reflecting from East Harlem on the impact of racism and injustice, he drew attention, before other contemporary theologians did so, to "the principalities and powers."[15] Racism and injustice in the systems are not simply matters of the heart, but powers that can only truly be addressed by challenging their idolatry, by learning the freedom to love.[16]

The powers represent the fall and are spread out through all domains of life. Stringfellow found them expressed in images, institutions, and ideologies.[17] While they are created powers, they are now demonic in nature, manifested as fallen social reality, including racism, predatory lending, unjust housing, schools that do not graduate children, and legal systems. The

---

14. Gutiérrez, *Theology of Liberation*, 35.

15. On his Harlem context, see Stringfellow, *My People is the Enemy*. While the entire corpus of his work addresses the powers, see especially Stringfellow, *Free in Obedience*; *Ethic for Christians*; and *Instead of Death*.

16. Stringfellow, *My People is the Enemy*, 148.

17. Stringfellow, *Free in Obedience*, 49–73.

powers think of themselves as gods, inverting what is intended for good for their own gain. Therefore, the powers as manifested in social reality can be aggressive, violent, and will turn on one another. Walter Wink called this the "domination system."[18]

While urban grace notes are not prominent in Stringfellow's outlook, he looked to Christ, and his victory of the powers, prominent themes in the Gospels, the Letter to the Ephesians, the Letter to the Colossians, and Revelation. This reflected Stringfellow's desire for a biblical outlook on politics and all of life. And it also required, in light of Christ's reconciling, the freedom to love oneself.

Perhaps the best commentary on the powers in the city is *The Wire*, David Simon's HBO drama where Sandtown is a part of Baltimore in which this story is set. Allan loved *The Wire*, a show that identified the urban political economy, and its institutions and ideologies, as part of a national and global story, playing out in real time in housing and public education, labor, markets, and the media.

Thanks to its development of characters such as Bodie, Omar, and Cedric Daniels, *The Wire* shows the ongoing "game"—the police and the drug trade—and how this is part of the city. It shows how the institutions of the city, such as government and education, can not only fail systematically, but can be corrupt, dismissive, exploitative, and aggressive in a manner most harmful to neighborhoods like Sandtown. And *The Wire* shows just how hard it is for people to break away from this cycle of violence, death, and the powers, for they can hold us in their thrall.

The death of Christ, René Girard helps us see, challenges the entire underlying system of violence, including the way in which Sandtown has been scapegoated.[19] The answer to the powers is not only their desacralization, but the witness of a new humanity set free from the powers to live for resurrection. As St. Paul writes, "through the church the wisdom of God in its rich variety might now be made known to the rulers and authorities in the heavenly places" (Ephesians 3:10). This is the gospel of which Saint Paul was a servant (Ephesians 3:7–9).

This witness to the powers begins, Stringfellow emphasized, with our baptism into Christ, our initiation into a new community, and continues with us learning to resist the powers through the way of the cross and the resurrection. Perhaps we need new language, and a deepened theology, to

---

18. Wink, *My Struggle to Become Human*.
19. Girard, *When These Things Begin*.

describe this task and calling, what Saint Paul calls "the ministry of reconciliation" (2 Corinthians 5:17–21).

In a beautiful and compelling way, the theologian Miroslav Volf does this. Drawing on his personal story formed in Croatia and by the realities of war, Volf invites us to be a people of embrace. In a world of exclusions, this means to take up the way of Christ and the cross in places of conflict and division.[20] It means to keep working at our relationships, language, and thought around context, theology, and formation.

The gospel helps us see that life is not meant to be a zero-sum world, a world of overwhelming competitiveness, of getting ahead at the expense of others. Such a way brings diminishment and loss, both to us and to all. Instead, as Rowan Williams asks us to consider in *Christ the Heart of Creation*, all of life is to be woven together in mutual blessing, a body in Christ. The ethical, the communal finds meaning in Christ.[21] Shalom—peace, well-being—is another way to say this. It is what God desires.

Being present in Sandtown was changing Allan. On January 25, 1988, after just a few days in the neighborhood, Allan composed a prayer in his journal that expressed his hope and way of responding to what was all around him. With rueful words, Allan prayed,

> *Father, forgive me and love me and break me, that I may be consumed with loving the poor surrounding me in response to the brokenness and love of Jesus on my behalf.*

Allan sought, he prayed for, a community that would be a sign in this neighborhood, however fragile, of a new humanity and of the re-creation of all things. A sign of Christ's presence. A community that would resist and interrupt the corrosive, divisive work of the powers that were at the source of Sandtown's injustice, by bringing people together in a different way that affirms the humanity of all—a community called New Song.

---

20. Volf, *Exclusion and Embrace*.
21. Williams, *Christ the Heart of Creation*.

New Song in front of a renovated 1385 North Gilmor Street, 1992
(Mark R. Gornik collection)

New Song crayon drawing (Mark R. Gornik collection)

Allan being transported to Baltimore Shock Trauma
(Tibbels Family, used with permission)

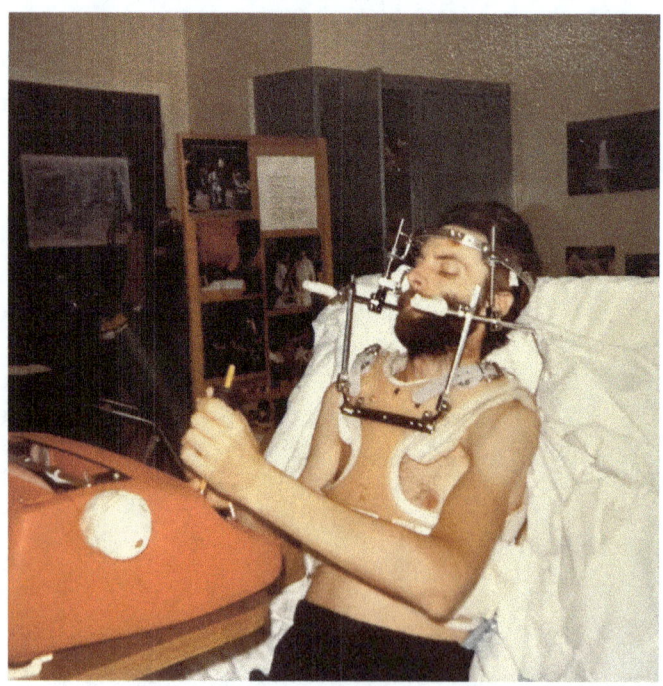

Allan in Baltimore Shock Trauma learning to type
(Tibbels Family, used with permission)

Checkers on a stoop in Sandtown (Roland Freeman, used with permission)

Ike at North Mount Street snowball stand, 2017 (Mark R. Gornik collection)

Mark as a very young pastor! With Tick and Allan (Mark R. Gornik collection)

Sunday on North Mount Street in front of our row house church. Good dog, Tungba! (Mark R. Gornik collection)

Eviction on North Mount Street (Mark R. Gornik)

Our future church home at 1385 North Gilmor, 1987 (Mark R. Gornik collection)

Ike posting a sign at 1385 North Gilmor (Mark R. Gornik collection)

Work underway on a first Sandtown Habitat house! (Mark R. Gornik collection)

Ella Johnson speaking at our first house dedication on March 4, 1990
(Mark R. Gornik collection)

Susan Tibbels and Linda Paige with Sandtown students
(Mark R. Gornik collection)

Reginald "Big Man" working in Sandtown (Mark R. Gornik collection)

Allan, Jessica, and Jennifer (Mark R. Gornik collection)

Jane Johnson (Mark R. Gornik collection)

John Perkins in Sandtown (Mark R. Gornik collection)

Prayerfully taking stock of the work ahead on the 1500 block of North Stricker Street (Mark R. Gornik collection)

Finished homes on 1500 block of North Stricker Street (Mark R. Gornik collection)

LaVerne Stokes, always on the job! (Mark R. Gornik collection)

Steve Fowl working on a house in Sandtown (Mark R. Gornik collection)

Elder Harris working for his neighborhood (Mark R. Gornik collection)

A Sandtown Habitat dedication on Fulton Avenue (Mark R. Gornik, collection)

Sonia Streets and Jimmy Carter, just the beginning of their work together! (Roland Freeman, used with permission)

John D and volunteers hard at work (Mike Barb, used with permission)

Nina in the Building Week tent (Mike Barb, used with permission)

Susan, Allan and Mark (Mark R. Gornik collection)

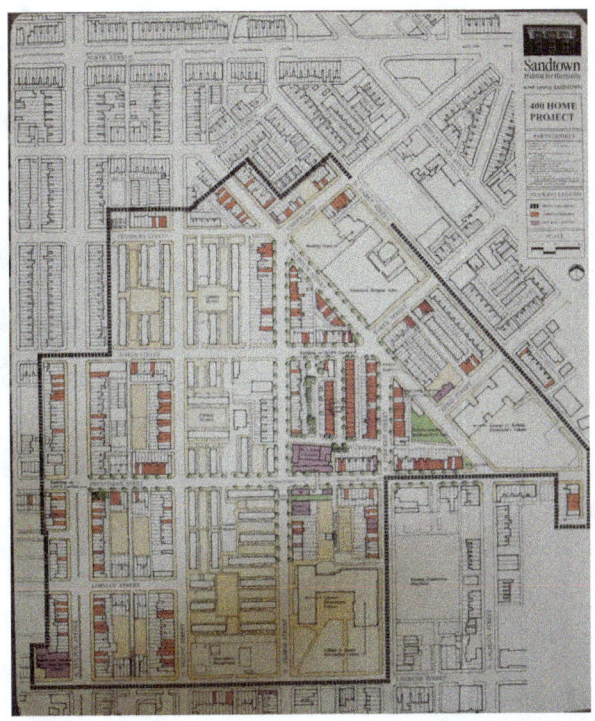

A map showing our four-hundred–house project and community initiatives in the fifteen-block focus area (Mark R. Gornik collection)

Pushing a shopping cart with recyclables in Sandtown (Mark R. Gornik collection)

Leslie Street before work began (Mark R. Gornik collection)

Leslie Street on dedication day for the entire block of new homes (Mark R. Gornik collection)

Leslie Street dedication (Mark R. Gornik collection)

Mark, Allan and LaVerne at Gilmor and Presstman (Mark R. Gornik collection)

Students reading in the library at New Song Academy (Mark R. Gornik collection)

Sonia Streets and Dr. "Ductman" Wessner at a morning devotion
(Mike Barb, used with permission)

Fitt Bennett in Sandtown (Mark R. Gornik collection)

Antoine Bennett speaking in Sandtown (Mike Barb, used with permission)

Students at New Song Center, where a vacant lot once stood
(Mike Barb, used with permission)

Don and Sarah Stevens-Rayburn and Danny Waid at a neighborhood dedication
(Mike Barb, used with permission)

Sandtown Habitat staff LeRoy (left) and Gary Mitchell (right)
(Mark R. Gornik collection)

Allan and Rodney Ross, 1988 (Mark R. Gornik collection)

Allan, LaVerne, and Sandtown Habitat staff (Mark R. Gornik collection)

Praying for the work of the Lord in the neighborhood
(Mike Barb, used with permission)

Allan at his home on Stricker Street (Mark R. Gornik collection)

Frank Ross in the neighborhood (Mark R. Gornik collection)

Mr. Kelley in the yard of 1385 North Gilmor, with New Song Center in the background (Mark R. Gornik collection)

Freeloaders Social Club, 2016 (Mark R. Gornik collection)

Mural honoring Freddie Gray on Mount Street (Mark R. Gornik collection)

Ike and his aunt Mamie Shaw on the day of her Sandtown Habitat House dedication (Mark R. Gornik collection)

Pastor Thurman Williams (Mike Barb, used with permission)

Patty Prasado-Rao speaking at a house dedication (Mike Barb, used with permission)

Mr. Charlie, Antoine, and Sean (Mike Barb, used with permission)

Winchester and Calhoun Street in Sandtown (Roland Freeman, used with permission)

On the stoop, 1989 (reprinted by permission from Baltimore Sun Media; all rights reserved)

Allan and Mark in Sandtown (Gabe Chen, used with permission)

Circle

On Sundays, we sat in a circle. Ike, Arteze, Anton, and Jermaine were there, and so was Big Man. Allan, Susan, Jenny, and Jessica came from two streets over, with neighbors like Shaconda and Nita. Mr. Ulysses Carter, who lived on the block and was our elder, joined in. The stoop was the overflow. Where Jesus is, this is church, not a collection of individuals, but something new that is already there by the call of God. The body of Christ.[1] In a circle, LaVerne came to a service and stayed because her children told her, "This is where Jesus is."

Our place of meeting was the front room of my unfinished house on Mount Street. The furniture was an old couch, some folding chairs, a repurposed box or two. Here we sat in a circle so we could see one another, listen to one another, read Scripture together. We sang songs like "People Get Ready," "We've Come this Far by Faith," "Holy Books," and "Sent by the Lord am I" from Central America. We prayed. We shared some food, maybe a cake. There was laughter, fellowship, community. And there was my dog Tungba, a very large black Labrador retriever, barking in the backyard, then bounding inside to help clean up any leftovers, nearly knocking us all over with his joy.

With music everywhere in the soundscape of the city, we called ourselves New Song. It helped that U2 had a song called "40," a reference to Psalm 40 that could be sung both as a celebration and a lament, a hymn that often closed out U2 shows. In Scripture, especially, a new song is something surprising, joyful beyond words. A new song was like Isaiah's "new thing" that God was doing, a new beginning, a new type of community, catching everyone off guard.[2]

---

1. Bonhoeffer, *Sanctorum Communio*.
2. A "new song" is a specific phrase in Psalms 40 and 98, and Revelation 5:9.

In fact, Christianity has always been best communicated through stories, parables, poems, watercolors, lives marked by mercy, and of course singing. One of the greatest theologians across history, the ancient Ephrem from Syria, understood this as he wrote theology through poems.

Few of us were talented vocalists at New Song, but here we were singing, our own work of God's art! It wasn't our voices, or the musicians we didn't have, but our small Christian community that was the choir and band of the New Song. This became its own metaphor for the living body God was building, the experience we had together of pardon and belonging, celebration and togetherness, singing and rejoicing. A prayer that we would be a new song.

New Song was more like a Latin American Base Ecclesial Community than a "traditional" church.[3] In our case, the *base* was our local reality, the neighborhood of Sandtown, a place from which to face reality from the bottom up. *Ecclesial* in this case refers to a new way of being church, to a holistic community, a place to nurture faith, and to read Scripture. And *community* refers to a place of sharing (the Greek word being *koinonia*) of ideas, gifts, and callings. Here was our context for prayer and Bible study.[4]

As John Stott describes in his commentary on Ephesians, the church is God's new society.[5] In Ephesians, we find that God's purposes for history is the reconciliation of all things under Christ, a new humanity (Ephesians 1:9–10, 2:11–22). For a living model of this reconciliation, we have the body of Christ, the church, a community of hope and praise before this work of God. This is where, and how, the powers are challenged. In all of this, there is prayer and praise before God.

Our life together did not develop around traditional roles, but around finding a common purpose in who we each were uniquely. As St. Paul reflects in 1 Corinthians 12, "just as the body is one and has many members, and all the members of the body, though many, are one body, so it is with Christ. For in the one Spirit we were all baptized into one body—Jews or Greeks, slaves or free—and we were all made to drink of one Spirit." As the gifts and callings of our small community began to blossom, as new energy emerged, it pushed our structures, even new as they were, to continually catch up.

---

3. Boff, *Ecclesiogenesis*; Cook, *Expectation of the Poor*; O'Halloran, *Living Cells*.
4. Cook, *Expectation of the Poor*.
5. Stott, *God's New Society*.

Small, local, urban church communities, depending upon the community for ministry, have long been the strength and life of the church (James 2:1–12; 4:5–6). In the first century, such communities started out in the alleys and byways of urban life, and in small tenement rooms, and these physical constraints limited the number of people in those communities. The first Christians were more neighborhood based than city focused; at the small scale is where faith was and is lived, challenged, and worked out.[6] The church was the parish, the local, as well as part of God's global story. A church, Stephen Bevans observes, that God is continually creating![7]

This journey, our community, was connected to the memory of God's work, to the story of Jesus in the Gospels of Matthew, Mark, Luke, and John, and the Acts of the Apostles. The early Christian churches, as Eduardo Hoornaert observes in *The Memory of the Christian People*, shared what they had, depended on divine miracles to get by, were led by women and people often considered by society to be insignificant, and thought through the intellectual basis of God's work in their lives and world.[8] In Christ they found a home marked by justice and mercy, a very different type of home and belonging than empire.[9]

Surely a mark of the Spirit, as Sister Joan Chittister points out, is laughter and joy.[10] So much of the Spirit's mark of joy in our midst was because of Allan, his laughter, his love for people, and the speed with which he rode toward you in his chair, watching you jump back as he abruptly but calmly stopped an inch away. It was also the picnics we had in parks, the sojourns to the Enoch Pratt Library downtown, the visits to Federal Hill and Fort McHenry, and the birthdays with fried cheese sticks and cake for everyone at Bennigan's restaurant in the Inner Harbor. Driving around the city, in Allan's van and my car, filled with neighborhood kids, listening to Public Enemy and Bruce Cockburn.

There were also the practical jokes in which we all took part, like decorating someone's house, inside and out, while they were away. Ike, Gary, Fitt, Jenny, and Jessica were all enlisted in such pranks, keeping the secret but unable to hide their delight. Or practical jokes like leaning a broom

---

6. Last, "Christ Worship in the Neighborhood," 310–25.

7. Bevans, *Community of Missionary Disciples*.

8. Hoornaert, *Memory of the Christian People*. See also Meeks, *First Urban Christians*; Kloppenborg, *Christ's Associations*; Crosby, *House of Disciples*.

9. See Keesmaat and Walsh, *Romans Disarmed*.

10. Chittister, *Radical Spirit*, 167.

against the door when someone went into the bathroom at my house or Allan's so that it would fall on the person as they came out. (How did we ever not know this was coming?)

A new vocabulary for church was being composed locally—love and friendship, neighborhood, and community. Words like *communion* and *sacrament* come closest to describing our experience together. Somehow God's acceptance without precondition, a sacrament of friendship, a communion was calling us together. God was inviting us to join in a choir, a new song of God sung in urban notes. As we sang this new song, we were being set free to serve God and our neighbors.

When the *Baltimore Sun* first wrote about our church, New Song, the headline was "Interracial Ministry Fused with Love." A few years later, another *Sun* story was titled "People Find a Voice with New Song" and "Christian Community is Moving Spirit of Sandtown Church." And nationally, CBS Sunday Morning with Charles Kuralt did a story on New Song that showed the life we were beginning to share.[11]

Just twenty-five years of age when I moved to Sandtown, it had not been my plan in life to be a pastor, only to serve Christ in the city. But here I was, a pastor. My first funerals and weddings, and much more, were struggles. I was learning about community building, the relationship of mission and ministry, the daily work of pastoral care. My experience and maturity were lacking.

Because pastoral ministry was the neighborhood, being present as a pastor to the whole community every day of the week, visiting with people in the homes, on the stoop, on the courts, in life, Sandtown was the seminary I needed.[12] Indeed, the neighborhood pastored me, formed me, and equipped me for ministry. Because of Sandtown, I learned the gifts that had been given me.

The important thing is to start where people are, where all of us are. If the emphasis of my theological tradition had been on acquiring and then delivering just the right words to answer the questions already in place, in Sandtown, by contrast, I learned that the primary theological task was to listen attentively—to my neighbors, to the questions of the community, and to the movement of the Spirit. What are people worried about?

---

11. Ercolano, "Interracial Ministry is Fused with Love" and Bock, "People Find a Voice with New Song." See also McDougall, *Black Baltimore*.

12. See the important work of the Learning Pastoral Imagination Project, including Scharen, "Learning Ministry Over Time."

CIRCLE

Happy about? Sad about? Angry about? Fearful about? Hopeful about? And not just listen but listen with my heart open to being changed. To God's abounding grace.

These questions helped me learn what the South African educator Anne Hope called "generative themes," meaning what matters most deeply to people.[13] I learned much about this approach in 1988 from Hope as she facilitated a "Training in Transformation" workshop in Washington, DC. The workshop not only helped me think about how we work for justice, and the role of dialogical learning stressed by Paulo Freire,[14] but also think differently around matters of organizational development, leadership, and planning for a different type of institutional life that reflects the people of the community.

Mamie Shaw and I lived on the same block of North Mount, our homes separated by an abandoned and collapsed shell of a row house. During times of hard rain, both of us could hear the floor beams and pieces of that house's roof groaning, sagging, and collapsing farther downward. We often sat together on one of our front stoops, or sometimes at her kitchen table or talked across the backyard fences, catching up on daily life, sharing a prayer.

Mamie has lived her whole life in Baltimore. Born in 1941, her father had been a minister, and she grew up with church services conducted in their home on Calloway Street. Mamie is Ike's aunt, and she not only houses Ike and his mother, but also her own children, Michael and Tanya. Moreover, she holds together an extended family that includes not only Ike, but Richard, Raymond, Jermaine, Shockie, Tick, and more people who turn to her to keep on going with life.

Mamie was always checking in on me. On holidays when everyone gathered at her house, she'd always make sure I had a bit of all the food prepared for a holiday family gathering on a plate filled to the brim and above.

Nothing came easy for Mamie, although I saw firsthand only a glimpse of the losses, frustrations, absentee landlords, and sufferings she endured, all entangled with race, gender, and location. But from Mamie, I see the gospel as good news (Luke 4:16–21), I hear about Jesus being with her, as he is with those who have "their backs up against the wall," as Howard

---

13. Hope and Timmel, *Training for Transformation*. For an account of her life, see Kilroe, *Anne Hope*.

14. Freire, *Pedagogy of the Oppressed*.

Thurman says.[15] I see how Mamie lives her faith in the "wilderness," how she sees God holding her story, making a way when there is seemingly no way.[16]

This is where the church needs to begin: with Mamie and a community of shared experiences of loss, lament, faith, hope, love, and reality. Here we find the wellspring of our sacred story. Not always or even most importantly the words we share, but the presence, the seeing of the face of one another.[17] This takes time, patience, risk. It requires being attentive to the story, to the countenance of one another. It requires a recognition that the community is often out in front of the church, but if our hearts are wide open like the doors of the church need to be, perhaps we can hear what is being said.

Pastoral ministry in Sandtown, I learned, was rooted in Jesus the Good Shepherd, who was proclaiming the love of God in his life and care. The ninth chapter of the Gospel of Matthew depicts Jesus as the good shepherd, present amidst danger and hardship, bringing the harassed flock to a flourishing life. This Jesus builds community with the harassed and forgotten. This Jesus is in Sandtown, pastoring the neighborhood. But the people of Sandtown are likewise carrying Jesus within them on the streets.[18]

As a cell is part of a larger body, whatever happened in Sandtown was part of our life as a body. This spoke to our pastoral work and priorities. One afternoon, Reginald (aka Big Man), then just a teenager who had earlier that day come to my house for our Bible study, was arrested on a misunderstanding. His arrest, and concerns about his physical condition while in custody, had me going back and forth between my home and the Western District police seeking information and his release. On one visit to the police station, I recall a hand-edited cartoon on the bulletin board. "The difference," between the Western District Police Station and the *Titanic*," it said, "was that at least they played music on the sinking ocean liner." This seemed to say it all about how the neighborhood was viewed.

We saw the same lack of concern in the health status of the neighborhood and more broadly in the health system's inadequacies and failures. One of my first encounters with the health system was with a man named Keith, who lived on the block. We had just met, and he wasn't feeling well,

---

15. Thurman, *Jesus and the Disinherited*.
16. See Delores Williams, *Sisters in the Wilderness*.
17. Ford, *Self and Salvation*.
18. See the image of Stephen Towns, "The Shepherd of Sandtown," 2014.

so I drove him to an emergency room in West Baltimore. Keith died the next day. He was so young, so were his children, and it was so sudden. His death impacted not only his family, but the block and neighborhood.

From then onward, I wondered about life and death disparities in the health care system. Services such as preventative and primary care were notably absent in Sandtown. And as I found by contacting Children's Defense Fund in Washington, DC, simple ways of learning about community health conditions can be a catalyst for understanding what needed to be changed.

This same Good Shepherd we found to be present amidst the gun violence in the neighborhood. Victims were always somebody's son or daughter, family member, neighbor. A part of a church. When Elnora, a deeply faithful member of our community, lost her second grandson to violence, the pain was unspeakable. We sat together, read Scripture, prayed, faced grief without words.

Sandtown has a very active theology of God as Good Shepherd. Invariably, at neighborhood funerals, the 23rd Psalm (King James Version) is recited from memory by nearly everyone present, whether they were formally a member of a church or not. This is what we prayed aloud together:

> The Lord is my shepherd; I shall not want.
>
> He maketh me to lie down in green pastures: he leadeth me beside the still waters.
>
> He restoreth my soul: he leadeth me in the paths of righteousness for his name's sake.
>
> Yea, though I walk through the valley of the shadow of death, I will fear no evil: for thou art with me; thy rod and thy staff they comfort me.
>
> Thou preparest a table before me in the presence of mine enemies: thou anointest my head with oil; my cup runneth over.
>
> Surely goodness and mercy shall follow me all the days of my life: and I will dwell in the house of the Lord for ever.

When Sandtown speaks or prays the words of Psalm 23, the neighborhood is declaring that in the face of troubles and pain God is the Shepherd. God is accompanying each family, a people, a neighborhood on its journey. This was a conviction that in the face of troubles and pain, "we will never walk alone." A belief that God loves Sandtown, but also a belief that in a world where death before its time was always near, that God intends life, joy, family, community, and friendship.

Despite what we were finding in our new community, and despite our practices being very much rooted in the New Testament story, our seemingly unconventional approach to church could be difficult to recognize for people with more traditional ideas and experiences of church. We realized, however, that church is life-changing when it begins with Christ at home in our lives, in our neighborhood. When the community of faith shares in the struggle for life and embraces the gift of the Spirit who brings new life.

But this requires freedom and space to grow. I could not see it as clearly then as I do now, but new wine really does need new wineskins, institutions in service of the gospel to support what is coming alive. That recognize the faith of a community and the presence of God.

Most of all, we were learning, as Rowan Williams describes, how to inhabit together such a new space, a change in atmosphere, God's dream within us, the world as new creation. "It is a place where we can see properly—God, God's creation, ourselves. It is a place or dimension in the universe that is in some way growing toward being the universe itself in restored relation to God."[19]

In Sandtown, we were being drawn into the life, dance, and circle of Father, Son, and Spirit. A circle of singing a new song.[20]

---

19. Williams, "Christian Priest Today."
20. O'Halloran, *Living Cells*.

Crayons

Sometimes all it takes to change a neighborhood are a few crayons, a sheet or two of newsprint, a poem, a biblical text, and a few dreamers.

One Sunday evening in 1988, our small community, mostly neighborhood kids and the senior and ever sartorial Mr. Carter, met in the front room of my row house on North Mount Street. We began by reading aloud a poem by Langston Hughes, "Harlem," about what happens when dreams are deferred because of injustice. Around the room, everyone knew this reality on the streets, in their homes, and at school. The poem became our cry, our prayer, a judgment to which we concurred.

Then we took turns reading aloud the second half of Isaiah 65. Here Isaiah announces a vision of a city and God's creation, where all things are new. There shall be no more weeping in sadness, infants will be born into health and each person will live their fullest years. People will rebuild the homes of their city and inhabit them. The work people do will bring forth the fruit of their hands, and the crown of it all will be joy. It is a picture of shalom, the wolf and lamb together in harmony. The peaceable kingdom.

We followed the reading of Isaiah with a question: Can you draw the vision of God for Sandtown, a vision you have for your family and neighborhood? Passing around crayons and spreading a large sheet of newsprint on the floor, we had people draw their answer—what they believed God intended for Sandtown, for their homes, their futures, their neighborhood.

The crayon image unfolds with simplicity and grace:

> *Vacant houses are no more. Empty storefronts are transformed into a bakery, a beauty salon, a grocery store, a car dealership, and a record shop. The neighborhood now has a health center, and children walk safely on the streets. Our church is in a reconfigured rowhome. New names claim the street signs. We are all there, present alongside one another. Even my dog Tungba is in the drawing.*

Sharing the Crust

In the drawing, where everyone has a job and a business, a home, health care, and experiences safety and a future with one another, we could see Pentecost with crayons. We could see what happens when "our sons and your daughters shall prophesy, and your young men shall see visions, and your old men shall dream dreams" (Acts 2:17). It was God's dream in us! It was Sandtown doing theology for the future, for life as God intends.

When we were done, when we had closed in prayer and we were all headed home, I rolled up the drawing and placed it atop my refrigerator for safe keeping.

If in Sandtown the obstacles to the wholeness of life that God intended were interconnected—food insecurity, limited transportation and access to jobs, an eviction epidemic, schools that did not send young people to high school, environmental degradation, death before its time—then this required a renewed vision of life together, of well-being and flourishing. The challenge called for an integral or holistic vision, what the Scriptures call shalom, the reconciliation of all things.[1] What we read in Isaiah.

No one else was going to do this for us, so we rolled up our sleeves and got to work, like we read in the book of Nehemiah. And yet, at that time none of us knew anything about housing, opening a health center, or developing a new school, and we certainly did not know where the resources would come from. But the Spirit of God had given us a vision, a dream, and we would figure out how to implement it as we went along.[2]

Every community needs a pedagogy, a way of learning. Rather than a pre-programmed plan, our approach was based on a pastoral cycle of reflection—action—celebration. This meant we would learn by doing, celebrate every little victory, and continually reflect on what occurred and what was next. We were walking together by faith, not sight, moving into a greater awareness of who we were becoming. Taking the time to live a process of growth with one another, to grow in depth of practice and wisdom, people and process, this is what mattered most, not programs, experts, or top-down approaches, religious or secular.

We started with what was right in front of us: *vacant houses*. Why not turn vacant and dilapidated houses into places of safety for homeownership by and for the people of Sandtown? And create jobs for the people of the community? As a precedent, we recalled the idea behind Habitat for

---

1. Wolterstorff, *Until Justice and Peace Embrace*.

2. Jeremiah 29:11. On the distinction between "planners" and "searchers," see the story of Partners in Health by Levy, "Poetry of Systems."

Humanity. The Habitat idea is for homes to be built by the local community at no profit and sold with no mortgage interest. It was a way of reclaiming the land and building community assets, and was an idea born at Koinonia, an interracial farming community in Americus, Georgia.

Founded by Clarence and Florence Jordan, Koinonia was committed to "the God movement," Clarence Jordan's term for the kingdom or reign of God, a vision for the here and now of the radical teachings of Jesus being realized in the Deep South.[3] The aliveness of the gospel was not only found in their farm, but in "The Cotton Patch Gospels," translations of the New Testament by Clarence Jordan. It was at Koinonia that Millard and Linda Fuller met the Jordans, and Habitat for Humanity was born. An expression of the "God movement" Clarence Jordan was writing about and working for, Habitat would become Millard's life work.

Calling from a pay phone at the downtown Bennigan's restaurant, Allan and I reached out to Habitat for Humanity headquarters in Americus, Georgia, asking to speak with Millard Fuller. To our surprise, Millard was in and took our call. After Allan explained who we were and our vision for our church to start a neighborhood-based Habitat affiliate, unique in the Habitat world, Millard asked whether we had one dollar and also whether we would be willing to pray for the work. Of course, Allan didn't have a dollar, but we did between us! And yes, we would pray. Millard's enthusiasm and support when we called was real and carried over for years, and he and Linda visited us often in Sandtown.

We were off and running, but our whole approach to renovating homes looked to many people outside Sandtown lost from the start. How could it not? None of us knew how to swing a hammer, hang dry wall, wire a new electrical system, repoint brick, or install a furnace. Not only that, but before we could get started, the owners of the vacant shells had to be found, and deals made to buy and then safely gut each so that a new home could emerge. Besides, we had no money.

But knowing our purpose and calling, knowing no one else was going to do it, we had no doubts. We believed we would find a way, that God would make a way. Although he himself could not hammer a nail, carry lumber, or walk up the steps to see inside a house, Allan could hear God's call, organize, and recruit people, pray, tell others the story, and gather funds.

---

3. For historical background, see Quiros, *God With Us*.

So, with a single vacant house finally purchased for a few thousand dollars on the 1600 block of North Gilmor Street, Allan and Susan's basement became the construction warehouse for the tools, materials, and supplies needed. We filled up his van with purchases from local lumber yards and hardware stores.

Frank, Fitt, Gary, Jon, Jenny, Jessica, Rodney, and everyone who could do so picked up a hammer, removed debris from the inside of the building, used a paint brush, and then eventually came to the dedication. People with other needed construction skills began to join in. Future homeowners put in hundreds of hours of sweat equity. As people came from all over to lend a hand, the work became a way for people to build relationships with people of different faiths, politics, geography, and background, to have true encounters, to find space to grow, to work for the common good.

It took more than a year, but a neighborhood family moved out of a high-rent and substandard apartment into a home they now owned. Mortgage payments would be around, or under, $300 per month. When our first house was completed, we celebrated with a dedication in the streets. There were testimonies, guests who spoke, the passing of a Bible and keys to the family, personal and communal prayers, a ribbon cutting, and singing "This Little Light." "All around the neighborhood," we were letting the light of the gospel shine!

Within just a few years, we had formally made it our goal to eliminate every vacant and abandoned house in a fifteen-block area of Sandtown, and to convert them to beautiful homes for neighborhood home ownership. No more renting a substandard home from an absentee landlord. No more unsafe living conditions. No more rental payments. The focus was on Calhoun, Baker, Stricker, Carey, Cumberland, Fulton, Gilmor, Laurens, Lorman, Mount, Presbury, Presstman, and School Streets, plus a whole block of new homes on Leslie Street.

When it comes to neighborhoods, it is easy to give up, pull away, or tear down what seems to not be working. But if we do this, we miss the memories, the history, the sanctity of place that people know as home.

The language and ideas of the urbanists Jane Jacobs and Roberta Brandes Gratz spoke to us: we were building on what's there, reweaving the urban fabric, working intuitively from the ground up, small changes combining to make big differences.[4] As Allan frequently pointed out, our efforts

---

4. Gratz, *Living City*; Jacobs, *Death and Life of Great American Cities*; Shepard, *City Makers*, 158.

to renovate and not tear down to start again was a green and ecological approach, in effect recycling materials for the well-being of the neighborhood and city.[5] It aligns with the importance of preservation of buildings, places, and institutions that is vital for our cities. This is a spiritual vision, and good work for the common good, as Elise Edwards has written.[6]

LaVerne Stokes, a leader of boundless wisdom, courage, and strength, began as a Sandtown Habitat homeowner, and then joined Allan as co-director of Sandtown Habitat. Born and raised in Sandtown, LaVerne was one of the first Sandtown Habitat homeowners, and was now rebuilding the very blocks where she had played as a child. She knew what it was like to live and raise a family in substandard rental housing, and what changing this would mean for her family and for the neighborhood.

LaVerne was not just building houses in her neighborhood but building up a community of love and justice. She was building a place marked by God's Spirit of "homefulness," which, as Brian Walsh sees, is not just housing, but life held together in wholeness and care.[7] Home as a place of belonging where we can be known for who we are, where we can live in safety and well-being, where we are supported to grow.[8] And LaVerne worked for all of this with prayer, kindness, and tenacity. She is a singular leader, gifted by God for her calling.

House by house, the work grew. And so did the staff, each person developing new skills and leadership in the community. In fact, Allan wanted to hire every young man in the neighborhood who needed a job. Within a few years, Gary Mitchell joined the staff, working in construction and painting. Orlando Mobuary headed a construction team and specialized in electrical systems. Ike kept track of everything, and he also worked in electrical. John Best was a construction manager. Mike Barb worked on administration, and at various points Bubby, Mary, Bo, Leroy, Frank, Danny, Denise, Barbara, Mark, and Andre joined the team.

Our goal was to not create programs, but to build community-based institutions that would build up, support, and sustain the neighborhood over time. At their heart, institutions like a hospital, library, gallery, store,

---

5. On seeing cities and development this way, see the inspiring story by Aguirre, "How to Recycle."

6. Edwards, "Womanist Consideration," and Soelle with Cloyes, *To Work and to Love*.

7. Bouma-Prediger and Walsh, *Beyond Homelessness*.

8. al-Sabouni, *Building for Hope*.

or even a restaurant, grow in capacity to do their work well, to grow and develop their vocation, to fulfill their purpose.

At their best, institutions like Sandtown Habitat and New Song are also covenants of love, ways the people of a community can express their hopes, wisely establish their shared goals, gather resources for the common good, and grow in knowledge, skills, and abilities to meet ever-changing challenges.[9] They exist in the present, but look forward to the future, to passing on a blessing to the next generation.

In the language of early Christians, the institutions we were creating were spaces of *diakonia*, service and justice; ways of following Jesus.[10] And institutions of *diakonia* create space for *koinonia*, avenues of sharing to achieve the common good. A housing corporation, a school, a health center, and more—each became a step, and a stepping-stone toward shalom.[11]

Neighborhoods need not only community institutions, but what the sociologist Eric Klinenberg calls social infrastructure—the physical spaces, buildings, and structures like libraries and schools that support and knit a community together.[12] They are vital physical spaces because they are places for people to gather and connect, to nurture families, safety, and growth. And from an architectural standpoint in Sandtown, they can build up and build on local memories and history.

Our social infrastructure work began at 1385 North Gilmor Street, located at the corner of North Gilmor and Laurens Street. A long-abandoned building in the middle of the neighborhood. Locally, it was known as "the mansion," for this was not just any abandoned building. Originally constructed in the nineteenth century as a private residence, for a time it was a Sisters of Mercy convent, serving nearby St. Gregory the Great Church. At both a slight topographical high point and centrally located in the neighborhood, by both its scale and location we knew it was to be the center of our community life. But getting it to a habitable point would take years.

The acquisition of this long vacant property became a crash course in urban real estate, and with seasoned advice from St. Ambrose Housing Aid Center, we found our way through the maze of banks, real estate

---

9. Hebrews 11:40, 12:1; 2 Thessalonians 2:15. In the New Testament, this is *paradosis*. My thanks to Luke Bretherton for pointing so clearly to this connection. See also 1 Corinthians 11:23.

10. Rowe, *Christianity's Surprise*, 55–80.

11. McDougall, *Black Baltimore*.

12. Klinenberg, *Palaces for the People*.

companies, speculators, building violations, and auctions. Step by step and dollar by dollar, after years of prayer and work we became the proud owners of 1385 and an equally abandoned adjacent carriage house. We had a sign made, borrowed a ladder, and then Mr. Ulysses Carter and Ike took turns climbing up and nailing that sign to the plywood, announcing "The Future Home of New Song."

The renovation of 1385 North Gilmor began when Ike, Bunky, Jermaine, Anton, and Arteze came to the building after school, figured out a way to clean it out, and worked together each day until dark. Thanks to Ellen Janes from the Neighborhood Design Center, soon a slew of volunteer planners, architects, and engineers, like Tom Gamper, joined the project. On Saturdays, Mr. White from the neighborhood would park his truck next to the building, wait for us to fill it up with debris, and then haul it away.

The first grant we received for the project was from The Abell Foundation, led by Robert (Bob) Embry. Thus began a friendship with Bob and the foundation, one that continued every step of the way that New Song traveled, and that involved learning from them and their care for Baltimore. Other people joined in the rebuilding—resetting the steps, repairing the floors, adding doors and windows, wiring the building, installing heat (but no air conditioning), adding bathrooms, plastering, and finally painting.

In an article about the dedication of the building, the *Baltimore Sun* quoted a neighbor as saying, "I think it's remarkable. It brings out something. I remember when it was a convent. It's good to see something happen in the community. We were so far down. We've come a long way."[13]

A school soon followed. Believing every young person in Sandtown to be a child of God who deserved a future of hope, Susan and neighborhood parents founded New Song Community Learning Center for neighborhood children and youth with a preschool, after-school program named "The After-Three Club" by Fitt. Camp was added to give kids a safe learning environment during the summer months. Wade and Ivy were among the first to enroll and Linda and Sonia were their first teachers. Within a few years, a public school, New Song Academy, was formed, ensuring that the future leaders of Sandtown would have the education they needed.

Supported by scholarship funds raised by Susan and the community, graduates of New Song Academy were placed in the best citywide high public schools, Catholic, and private schools. Along the way there were programs in gardening with Irvine Nature Center, music that came through

---

13. Khalid, "Neighborhood Celebrates."

a partnership with the Baltimore Symphony Orchestra, extended school hours, and an extended (year-round) academic year. High school students continued with New Song as mentors and continued to receive support after school. The next stop was college.

As a leader, Susan was not just visionary and compassionate, she was also committed to developing the inherent educators around her. To this end, she built a teaching staff drawn largely from within the neighborhood, investing in their professional development. And together, they worked closely with each student to know their learning needs, supporting their family stories.

Jane Johnson became the co-director and later director of New Song. Jane loved the kids, and having grown up in the neighborhood and raised her family here, knew their context. She was always on duty, caring, being a witness. Born of love and respect for each student, Jane, Susan, and the entire staff had high standards that opened untold doors of life opportunity for them.

The vision and approach of New Song Academy worked because of dedicated people like Mr. Kelley, who oversaw the building and operations; Chrystal Boykins and Trina Davis at the front desk, and Sean Stevenson, gym teacher and basketball coach; teachers like Mary Lee Williams, Paula Huggins, Louise Paige, Jenny Wiggins, Mrs. Kelley, and Emily Maunz-Marcus; Breai Mason-Campbell, who taught dance; and Tolu Sosayana, who came to Sandtown from Duke Divinity School and helped young people prepare to attend college.

The experiences of our neighborhood led us to also begin community health programs and eventually primary care.[14] Bracingly high rates of diabetes, hypertension, asthma, HIV/AIDS, and low infant birth weights were serious challenges in the neighborhood. As renowned physician Paul Farmer emphasized, this is a faith and a social justice issue.[15]

The first health action we took was to work with Johns Hopkins School of Public Health, developing a small team of people trained to go door-to-door identifying people with hypertension, and then if a need or concern arose, directing such neighbors to providers around the city.[16] It was low

---

14. See the work of John W. Hatch, including "General Baptist State Convention Health and Human Services Project."

15. Farmer, *Pathologies of Power*.

16. Gunderson et al., "Faith-Based Assets," 236–37.

cost, low tech, and, from what we could tell, highly effective. Eventually, we were able to provide limited primary care using volunteer physicians.

A holistic community model of health care was coming into place, and in a few years we established a full-time health center, advancing health equity. We were profoundly blessed that the health center was led from the start by Dr. David Thomas, a leading internal medicine and infectious disease expert at Johns Hopkins. Dave would come in the evenings and care for patients who had no other access to health care. In later years, Dr. Belinda Chen would also provide vital leadership. With their spouses Suzanne Thomas and Gabe Chen, they gave their gifts and callings to the health and well-being of Sandtown.

Journaling from the vantage point of almost twenty years later, it is clear that Allan had a strong sense of how the community-based approach—one family, one house, one block at a time—worked, would gain momentum, and could influence how society saw Sandtown, the city.

In an entry from his journal dated December 12, 2008, Allan first identifies what the existence of Sandtown says about America, and gives his social and political judgment:

> *If how a nation treats its most vulnerable citizens shows the character of that nation, the United States is in trouble; Baltimore is in trouble.*

Allan then follows with a summary of what the neighborhood approach looks like and his commitment:

> *The revitalization of the "severely distressed" neighborhoods is out of vogue, has been for quite a few years now, but we will continue our house by house and block by block plan through the 30 years we originally committed. In the end the people who were living here will still be living here, most of them now in homes they own or have passed on to their children, with their children attending an academically excellent school and many others having graduated from college, and they will purchase their coffee in the morning from a neighborhood resident-owned corner store and perhaps eat dinner at a neighborhood resident-owned sit-down restaurant. The residents of Sandtown are not throw-away citizens; they love their lives and their neighborhood and desire to see it rebuilt and thriving.*

This, for Allan, goes to the purpose of the church, namely faith, hope, and love in action:

Sharing the Crust

> *New Song exists for this purpose, to be partners in the realization of these dreams. The process will be messy, with many setbacks along the way; the blocks will be noisy with the sound of many children playing in the streets in which they feel secure, and at times their football or basketball will inadvertently break the glass of a car or building. But the end result will be one born of dignity and moral clarity, and the joy will be authentic and the depth of character of the neighborhood real.*

Allan had an expectation that Sandtown could become more just, more in line with God's purposes for all of creation.

A decade after our evening of planning with crayons, poetry, and Isaiah 65, atop my refrigerator and stuck behind expired cereal boxes, I happened upon the drawing we had created. Unrolling the thin and now aged paper, the crayon lines, and images yet before me, I could see that almost the entirety of the vision had been realized. God had given us the freedom to join in the kingdom, to labor together, to change history one house, one block at a time.

But looking at the crayon drawing again, I can now see it wasn't just a vision, but a map. A map of how people lived and moved about in their neighborhood. The middle school-aged artists knew they could not just fix up houses, because that is now how they lived on their blocks. They needed a home for worship, places to shop, a doctor to see, sidewalks to get around. A map of where we were going.

"I know the dreams I have for you, says the Lord, plans for your peace and not for harm, to give you a future with hope."[17] God was dwelling with us and at home, and we were dwelling with God and one another, with all of creation, living in peace. Dreams of the Spirit revealed with crayons.

---

17. Jeremiah 29:11.

Loaves

As I reflect back and forth over the years, I now recognize that at the heart of our efforts in Sandtown was creating a new economy, an economy based on loaves and fishes. Starting small, beginning with what we had, our loaves and fishes, we found a life of abundance not scarcity. Where everyone has something to give and receive, and we grew together.

From sharing bread with one another, to meeting Jesus over a meal, we then looked forward to the feast that is to come, the kingdom that Jesus proclaims is about food and meals together (Luke 13:29).[1] I love that loaves and fishes may not only have been a favorite meal of Jesus, but it is a favorite meal for Sandtown, with "Lake Trout" available from many a carry-out corner store!

The story of the loaves and fishes, recounted in each of the Gospels, begins with a crowd gathered to be near Jesus, to learn from him and to experience healing. But by the end of the day, the people are hungry and in need of sustenance, of food.

At first, however, the disciples suggest to Jesus that everyone should be sent home. They think that nothing much can be done, that the expense of feeding them all will be too great. But Jesus takes a different approach, beginning with what they have, five loaves and two fish. In the Gospel of John, they come from a boy, who gives Jesus what he has. Jesus then blesses this offering of loaves and fishes. As the food is distributed, it generates not only enough to feed thousands, but a surplus of bread and fish. Whereas the disciples see only scarcity, limits, Jesus sees abundance, and the people are nourished by food, a sign of God's new life.

These loaves and fishes represent an economy based on the continual circulation of gifts, for the flourishing of all. Rather than extraction, a loaves

---

1. Croasmun and Volf, *Hunger for Home*.

and fishes economy in Sandtown connects to the regenerative and life-giving energies of the neighborhood that continually circulate for the basics of life and that aim for community-based ownership of housing, land, and basic life goods. It is an economy rooted in the traditions of the Jubilee and Sabbath year described in the Hebrew Scriptures, a view that maintains that all resources come from and belong to God.

Let's remember the economic challenges facing Sandtown. With no neighborhood-owned stores or businesses, economic resources spent in the neighborhood rarely stayed in the neighborhood. Rental payments, utility bills, money spent at corner stores: all this and more flowed outside the neighborhood, the wealth settling into other parts of the city and region.[2]

One sign of the local economy was people pulling or pushing a shopping cart on the streets, filled with gathered bottles, cans, or metals like copper drawn from abandoned houses, headed to nearby scrap yards or recycling centers. Here were our neighbors who couldn't find other jobs. This wasn't what it should be, but it was part of a recycling economy in many neighborhoods, and it showed how hard people were working to support their families.

Few people owned their homes, and therefore few passed along such an important asset to their families. Mortgages from banks were unthinkable, and private investment was scarce. The rare "salesmen" visiting the neighborhood were going door to door selling burial insurance. Transportation networks, necessary for mobility, for work and travel, were among the worst in a city that even overall does not do well.

In an economy of loaves and fishes, you never begin with nothing: there is always something.[3] As we also see in the New Testament, the church is about gifts for the body and about service rather than status and acquisition.[4] As St. Paul writes in 1 Corinthians 12:4–7, "Now there are varieties of gifts, but the same Spirit; and there are varieties of services, but the same Lord; and there are varieties of activities, but it is the same God who activates all of them in everyone. To each is given the manifestation of the Spirit for the common good."

"For the common good" in Sandtown means that each of us—like Ike, Susan, Frank, LaVerne, Nina, Allan, Fitt, Gary, Antoine—had a gift, a

---

2. Shelton, "Rethinking the RECAP."

3. John McKnight has long emphasized the importance of the local community as a rich resource. For example, see McKnight and Block, *Abundant Community*.

4. See Snyder, *Liberating the Church* and *Community of the King*.

grace for the well-being of Sandtown, one another, and our neighbors. As the gifts and callings of our small community began to blossom, we also discovered that, as we read in Ephesians 4, with that blossoming something new happens within each of us, together, around us: the energies of the Spirit of life burst forth.

Rather than build a ladder of development for one or the few, we sought to create a community where everyone could climb further together. Such solidarity, of growing and moving ahead together, is a priority of the way of Jesus and the justice of the kingdom of God.[5]

As I think about it, Allan, Susan, and I could not even have started out without such sharing and caring for one another. To move to Sandtown, we pooled our resources, helping one another with all we had. While going through some old files, I was reminded that Allan and Susan had paid much of the first years of my small salary out of their own limited resources. This is but one way that Allan and Susan made my calling possible, something we continued for one another. And they did this for neighbors too, a circle of mutuality and grace.

To my knowledge, we became the largest employer in Sandtown, and sent young people off to college for the first time in their family. Everything we did, from the school, the health center, an employment program called EDEN Jobs, and more contributed to creating a new economy.

But the backbone of our long-term economic approach was housing. As we saw it, vacant houses were not "investment opportunities," but a future for the people who were already living in Sandtown. The work of homebuilding created family and neighborhood assets and healthy environments. Moreover, it addressed the underlying challenge that, without ownership, the neighborhood was rendered nearly landless. In fact, "ground rent," a holdover from the British land system, was still required on many properties. Sandtown Habitat not only built homes, but created jobs, skills, and shared accomplishment.

Like loaves and fishes, the monthly mortgage that the owners of each Sandtown Habitat home paid we recycled back into the community, helping to fund the next house. This in turn created jobs in the neighborhood, and this is why Sandtown Habitat became a driver of economic development.

In 1992, President Jimmy Carter and Rosalynn Carter decided to come and work in the neighborhood with Sandtown Habitat. Our admiration for the Carter's commitment to human rights, conflict resolution, the

---

5. Cook, "Protestant Predicament."

environment, global public health, and much more was profound. It was determined that the Carters would work on one house. Building on this opportunity, we announced a one hundred-home project, starting with ten homes that week, even though at that point we had only completed three houses, had no money, and only one staff person!

For the Carters' visit, we held a building week that was one part revival, the other part hard hats and dumpsters. We set up an open-air tent nearly the size of a city block for morning singing, biblical reflection by local pastors, and announcements. Everyone got a Sandtown Building Week T-shirt.

Elder Clyde Harris, who with his wife Amelia Harris was pastor of what was then called Newborn Apostolic Holiness Faith Church of the Trinity, was energized by the life of faith and care for the neighborhood in which he'd grown up. It was with such passion he dispersed us each morning during the Carter work week, shouting, *"Are you ready? Are you ready? Let's get to work!"*

The Carters worked on Sonia's home on North Gilmor Street. They would become friends, and Sonia later would join the Carters working around the world on Habitat projects. To close their time in Sandtown, we held a worship service at New Shiloh Baptist Church that filled their sanctuary. President Carter spoke, preached really, from 2 Corinthians about what matters, what lasts in life, what is eternal. The gifts we are given and called to use.

Jimmy and Rosalynn Carter were incredible and worked harder than anyone. You could really see their Christian faith lived out. Their work in Sandtown, and gracious spirit, was just the catalyst we needed, even as we nearly collapsed from exhaustion getting ready and then through the week. After finishing one hundred homes over the next few years, we then launched a four-hundred-home project, a number that would eliminate vacant homes in our fifteen-block focus area.

Because the building week with the Carters went so well, we repeated the process of building weeks, Summer Building Week, as it became known. We held a building week or two each summer, tent on the lot and all, though physically without the Carters, but with their spirit, and with themes like Building on Hope, Building on Faith, and Building on Love. This was our theology. And of course, every year had a new T-shirt with the theme, and soon, we could see our T-shirts all over the neighborhood, even randomly around the city. By my count, over time, I'm sure we made and distributed over ten thousand Sandtown Habitat and New Song T-shirts!

How the resources came together to build that first home, and then even more homes, was itself part of the new economic cycle of loaves and fishes taking place. Steve Fowl, a New Testament theologian at Loyola University and a member of the Episcopal Cathedral of the Incarnation, had been coming regularly to work in Sandtown. Following his day at Loyola, Steve would show up in Sandtown to work on houses, doing whatever was needed. Soon Steve got the cathedral to sponsor a house, and to work alongside a neighborhood family, a pattern repeated and led by Sarah and Don Stevens-Rayburn and Pastor Van Gardner for nearly twenty years.

As a result, many more churches of all denominations become involved in rebuilding Sandtown in a program we called "one church, one home." Lutheran, Presbyterian, Episcopal, suburban, rural, evangelical, and mainline churches joined together in Sandtown, each church helping to build one home. Students from Loyola University also became involved in building homes, as did others from as far away as Connecticut with the youth group of Pastor Skip Masback. Nearby Bethel AME invested in three homes for families, an exciting partnership right in the neighborhood. And then there was John Wessner, who played the trombone at every dedication and installed the furnace system that went into each and every Sandtown Habitat home.

You just have to get started!

Partnerships made the work in Sandtown possible and go further. We had countless friends, local foundations, churches, and agencies who went above and beyond. The Enterprise Foundation, founded by Jim and Patty Rouse, inspired by Jim's encounter with Church of the Saviour and the pastor Gordon Cosby in Washington, DC, was key in expanding and deepening the work in Sandtown Habitat, especially through loans that supported costs around construction before the sale of each home. Bert Hash and MECU also helped with the mortgages and neighborhood banking. Building on a community base, Mayor Schmoke and the City of Baltimore became partners, as did local corporations like Black and Decker. And nearby, BUILD also developed houses.

Rather than decide to stop at a certain point—say after a hundred or three hundred houses—we kept asking ourselves: How can we use what we have now to go further and deeper into our calling? This was our own reading of the parable of the talents.

As each project was completed, we immediately made use of our newly developed asset by leveraging it for whatever was next. Shortly after we dedicated 1385 North Gilmor Street, our home, we mortgaged it and used the money to buy a block of vacant houses on North Sticker Street for Sandtown Habitat. LaVerne worked hard negotiating and then closing this deal. Within a few years, the Stricker Street block became lined with beautifully rebuilt housing with a palette of pastel facades.

We were learning that the biggest risk is often not what we don't have, but not using what we have been given for the "more good," for the fullest, deepest potential. To do all we could to build up a more sustainable community. This abundance, this new economy is what John Perkins called "redistribution," an economic notion more radical in Christian nature and implication than we may realize. It was about people developing economic assets, earning a high school diploma, a college degree, focusing on their health and well-being. All of this builds up a new economic life. All of this was because we shared our loaves and fishes in Sandtown.

When we share, there is "enough for all," (Acts 2), and both the "enough" and "all" keep growing! We were on a journey toward what more—what common good—can be in a neighborhood.[6] The more—the possibility—lay in the energy of creation and our work together. And like the eucharistic loaf, loaves and fishes remind us that while we are indeed all broken and scarred, we, even a neighborhood and city, can also be made whole.

A loaves and fishes approach trusts God to make a way when there is seemingly no way. Take the vacant lot that sat across the street from 1385 North Gilmor, for instance. Even though we had no money and had just started the after-school program, we could envision a school rising there one day. So, with the help of family and friends, we pulled together the funds, and I went to the closing with the checks that were needed. However, when the final numbers were calculated, we learned the closing costs had risen.

I tried not to show my concern, but there were no other funds to make up the difference in any account, personal or ministry. The attorneys quietly conferred with one another, and then they announced that the seller's attorney was paying the difference, and so the deal was closed. A few years later, a beautiful community center arose called New Song Center, a home for New Song Academy complete with classrooms, gym, cafeteria, library, and roof garden.

---

6. Moltmann, *Source of Life*.

Loaves

In freedom to be generous from the gift that is Christ,[7] to meet the needs of others with the abundance we have, we were finding an economy of interdependence, sharing, abundance, and sustainability (2 Corinthians 8–9). With loaves and fishes, we began to form relationships that turned away from our own resourcefulness to the way Christ relates to us for the world to work.[8] We weren't dreaming outside the box so much as inside the kingdom of God.[9]

Grace upon grace, block by block, we found that what it takes to begin to create a new urban economy is imagination, love for one another, friendship, hard work, prayer, sharing our loaves and fishes, more hard work, and of course, with Sandtown Habitat and New Song T-shirts for all!

---

7. For important discussions on the role of gift in Paul, see Fowl, *Philippians*, and Barclay, *Paul and the Gift*.

8. Williams, *Christ the Heart of Creation*.

9. Boyle, *Barking to the Choir*.

Birds

God is a God of surprises. Among them, perhaps chiefly for someone from Baltimore, who grew up with pictures of Baltimore Orioles players on my bedroom wall, I became a New York Yankees fan. When my baseball conversion occurred, Allan raised questions about my faith, and announced this to anybody who would listen. I understand that on principle, many agree with him! This became a source of much conversation in Sandtown, the Yankees part of it at least. But as with any conversion, it is perhaps more interesting to ask, how did it happen?

Being a pastor in Sandtown was not so much a job as a commitment to the community and the gospel, integral to the life God had given me. It was about accompanying people in life, from their losses to their new beginnings, with everything in between. I loved being in the neighborhood and living on Mount Street. Each day as a pastor was humbling, a gift, a blessing.

But God's picture is bigger than my imagination, and while I had expected to be in Sandtown for the foreseeable future, unexpectedly, I experienced the Spirit calling me to begin again in ministry in a new urban setting, New York City. After almost a decade of the joys and challenges of pastoral and community work, the timing seemed right.

A key reason New York became possible was because of friends like Tim Keller, who had been my professor in seminary and who was now the pastor of Redeemer Presbyterian Church. He believed in our work in Sandtown and encouraged me to come to New York. Tim understood the complexity of the city and its possibilities for manifesting the power of the gospel. He knew me and encouraged me.

I was not going alone, but with Rita. A family physician working in West Baltimore when we met, Rita's story and family were rooted in Hungary, a nation not long released from Soviet occupation. In my first visit to Budapest, I was introduced through her family to Taizé, an ecumenical movement of prayer, trust, and community based in France that was affecting young people across Europe. When God granted Rita and me two sons, Peter and Daniel, they grew up as New Yorkers speaking Hungarian and English at home. Yankees fans, of course. And all in on the Knicks.

At our December wedding at the Episcopal Cathedral of the Incarnation in Baltimore, we included a reading from the late Archbishop of El Salvador, Oscar Romero. "As the Magi from the East followed their star and found Jesus, who filled their hearts with boundless joy, let us too, even in hours of uncertainty, of shadows, of darkness like those Magi had, not fail to follow that star, the star of our faith."[1] Together, we would seek to follow the star of our faith in our vocations and family.

In the summer of 1998, our North Mount Street home now emptied and the moving van pulling away, Rita and I stood on the sidewalk with Ike, Jermaine, Mac, and others from the block. With gratitude for the blessings of our neighbors and for our shared life, and with many tears, Rita and I got into our car, headed down Mount Street, and then onto Route 40, MLK, and then I-95 north to New York. It was another step in our journey of holding the joys we had received and letting go of the griefs in order to follow Christ in trust.[2] The Spirit was moving us to New York (Isaiah 55:9).

Initially our new church and work was going to be in the South Bronx, but our path was turned to Harlem. We moved to New York to work with our friends Jeff and Rebecca White, and to help see the launch of a second New Song. Jeff would be our pastor. Knowing and being blessed by his pastoral skill and commitment to people and church life, we were grateful.

But leaving Sandtown had not been without its difficulties and second thoughts. As such personal changes often do, they awakened in me a sense of inadequacy, shame, failure, woundedness. There were many things I felt had been blessed during my time in the neighborhood, and there were things I would have done differently. But at many moments I now felt like the disciple Peter out on the water, going under when I looked back instead of forward to Christ.

Just after 9/11, my friend Peter Price, who was newly appointed as the Bishop of Bath and Wells in England, visited us for an extended stay before beginning his new role. Having come to Sandtown many times, Peter knew our story well, and recognized, as did Rita, that I was carrying with me

---

1. Romero, *Violence of Love*, 40–41.
2. For the theme of discernment, see Ivens, *Keeping in Touch*, 74–75.

painful burdens from Sandtown. Forming and caring for communities can happen at great personal cost, and those things can affect a pastor in ways that cannot always be understood or shared with others (1 Corinthians 4:1–13).

Bishop Peter knew that a spiritual director, someone who could walk with me to discern the movements of the Spirit in my life, would be crucial to my well-being and future in ministry, and he arranged for me to meet with Sister Grace at Maryknoll. Some years later, I learned that part of Sister Grace's unique calling and gift is to be with people who have experienced a major disruption, a trauma in their life and ministry, and who need to consider their story in a new way.

Talking with Sister Grace, I came to see that what I believed were my "failures" in Sandtown were part of my story, and that I could learn from them and integrate them into my life. The wounds, shame, guilt, and sometimes anger I held were not only making me spin my wheels but were hindering God's new dream for my life from coming into being.

I came to recognize Christ's suffering and resurrection in my own life, and to recognize that dying could be a grace. The unknown I had faced that had brought such suffering could also be an invitation to live with forgiveness, trust, and joy. A freedom that I had not considered or perhaps even experienced; it was a realization that I was free to carry my calling further. It was an invitation to become more fully myself in Christ, to shape me for whatever was next.

What is essential, Sister Grace said to me, *is to be rooted in the realm of Love.* The heart and mystery of God, Love, she emphasized, is not as much a feeling or virtue but a revelation of God coursing through the creation and across our lives, connecting everything. Love is the horizon of communion, of our presence, our journey, our service. It is wholeness and healing. Love is the love of the Father, Son, and Spirit in communion with all.

In and for Love is where we are most fully alive, as St. Paul writes in Ephesians 3:14–19. Perhaps I could hear it too, like John Coltrane's "Love Supreme," I thought, its chords expansive and with an unexpected style, filling, drawing the world of the listener into its own mystery. Perhaps something important here resonates with the theologian of creation and mystery Pierre Teilhard de Chardin.

I remember well that before my first meeting with Sister Grace had even ended, I could feel healing take place in my body, and desolation becoming consolation. That moment marked the beginning of my recognition of the mystery of communion and Love in and all around me, my "inner being," as the psalmist put it (Psalm 51:6).

This consolation became how I was able to live out my calling, gaining a deeper love in Christ and service to God, an openness to receive the new community God had given me. I could now re-enter life in New York and ministerial service through a deepening communion of Love. I had a newfound freedom to grow with and from others, to regain my own trust, not to reject my own call and vocation. And to grow through new friendships, as a result of what I had learned from Sandtown.[3]

I recognize that none of us fully knows ourselves, and that there are many layers of emotional and social complexity to our lives and stories, as also to the lives and stories of those with whom we interact. But as I would later learn from Sister Grace and Ignatian spirituality, doubts, even strong doubts, are not uncommon when one is facing a significant change in ministry and life. There is not just the will, but our emotions and ways we think. I needed a clearer recognition of my own grace, of my inner calling, and of my service. I needed to stay with my experience, as Sister Grace emphasized.

If we are open to change, we can often learn the most from what doesn't work out the way we hoped, the hard stuff that happens in ministry. Given a choice, I would not have gone through this process of suffering that had spanned many years and brought with it many personal sorrows. But God used these experiences in my life as a grace, helping me find my life truly in Christ, and helping to move me in directions I would otherwise not have gone. I was now more attuned to the dynamics of a community's life, especially at points of growth and change, and the different types of transitions and concerns that pastors, other leaders, and communities face all the time.

Going forward, I also found wisdom in a more Ignatian way of proceeding, for making decisions and working.[4] This way of discernment depends upon inner freedom and on a clarity that we learn from God's purposes in the context of seeking the reign of God. It depends on our attentiveness to the whole of what is going on around us in the world. I needed to trust that God was opening a new space in my life, giving me

---

3. See Nouwen, *Inner Voice of Love*.

4. A critical work is Brackley, *Call to Discernment*. For an introduction to discernment and the Jesuits, see Martin, *Jesuit Guide*.

new friends to share in the work of the reign of God, people who would shape my life. I needed to recognize that this was the Spirit at work, a gift, an invitation to new life. Doors closing in one place really could mean new possibilities in another.

Yet if the compass rose had brought us to New York City, it was not for the reasons we had first expected. And if we had envisaged staying in New York for only a few years, that changed too. Being present to experience all around us began to show me this.

It turned out, contrary to reports, Christian faith wasn't dying in New York: it was thriving! With migration joined to urbanization, a global church closely connected to cities like Lagos and Accra, Seoul and Hong Kong, Sao Paulo and Mexico City was growing in the neighborhoods of New York.[5]

From my first days in Harlem, I noticed West African immigrants, primarily from Senegal, Ivory Coast, Mali, Ghana, and Guinea and their shops like A G Fashion and Touba Service Center. The music of the singular Senegalese artist Youssou N'Dour always seemed to be playing in the local coffee shops, park sidewalks, and stores. Aware that Christian faith was growing in Africa, I wondered whether among the new African immigrant population in New York there was also a Christian community, and if so, where they were worshipping.

To understand this new African diaspora, immigration, and even wider demographic movements within Christianity and the city, I found myself reaching out to Andrew Walls, who was from Aberdeen, Scotland, but who was then a visiting professor at Princeton Theological Seminary. It was Walls who first identified and wrote about this shift in Christianity from the West to the non-Western world, and its meaning for the church, Christian scholarship, and mission.[6]

With a Metro card for the subway and bus transportation, and a lot of walking, I began worshipping with a range of new African and other diaspora churches. Sundays now became my classroom into a world of Christianity, its preaching, worship, families, prayers. Understanding these changes in the city, church, and ministry, as I learned from Walls, was not a matter of adding in bits of new demographic and numerical information to existing frameworks, but something more joyful, more theologically and spiritually challenging.

---

5. Gornik and Liu Wong, *Stay in the City*, and Gornik, *Word Made Global*.
6. For an introduction to Andrew F. Walls, see his *Missionary Movement*.

Rather than putting the West at the center implicitly or explicitly, Walls saw it was essential to learn Christ from one another, a vision of the church that Walls saw grounded in St. Paul's letter to the Ephesians.[7] Out of this vision, and in close friendship and generosity of spirit, Walls became involved in helping us to shape a vision for a new institution in New York that would respond to this changing ecclesial reality.

In response to the joyful thing that God was doing in our city, we formed City Seminary of New York as an intentional seminary for our city. The goal of the seminary was to serve the church that was thriving in New York but did not generally have access to a larger community of mutual learning, and also one with appropriate curriculum and pedagogy for the city. This is why to me theological education is a justice issue. Urban church leaders should not be left out because of their neighborhood location, theological background, or resources.

But City Seminary would become much more. It would become a community of caring deeply for one another, a way of bringing together the diversity of the body of Christ from across neighborhoods. It would be a source of joy and growth, a sign of hope and life, a place to work out ministry practice. Like church life in New York, City Seminary would be experiential and rooted in theological reflection around family, pastoral, and congregational life. The Word in our midst, in the city.

As in Sandtown, there was no grand plan and few traditional resources in place on which we could draw, so instead we had to build the seminary from the ground up, based on the gifts and life of our community, the questions and dynamics of our city. Vulnerability—depending upon God—was crucial, for it opened us to see that God was bringing together something only God could do. Prayer was the only way we could proceed, as we would find our own calling and approach to theological education.

City Seminary would not be possible without friendship. Joining Andrew Walls in walking with us was Manny Ortiz and Sue Baker, founders and pastors of Spirit and Truth Fellowship in Philadelphia. They became mentors and co-workers for the seminary in this new urban setting, with deep pastoral experience. Manny and Sue supported and stayed with me, helping to do what was needed to establish a seminary for Christ's mission, no matter the time and effort it took.

Bruce and Marjie Calvert joined us in this effort of establishing City Seminary. With the eyes of faith, and in care and friendship, Bruce and

---

7. Walls, *Cross Cultural Process*.

Marjie saw potential for having an impact in the city through the seminary, and we walked together in that calling. Tim Keller was encouraging along the whole of our journey too.

God is present in bringing things together, like how Maria Liu Wong and Miriam Acevedo jumped in, each with foundational gifts of vision, leadership, and commitment, sharing in the hard work of institution building and community life. They were the friends that I needed for life and mission.

We were soon joined by Bola Oyesanya, Derrick Miu, Vivian and Beverly Grubb, Geomon and Reji George, Adrienne Croskey and her extended family in Harlem, Sister Marylin Gramas, Adebisi and Abby Oyesile, Huibing He, Sarah Gerth van den Berg, Robert McInnis, Kari Jo Cates, Tony Wong, Peter Acevedo, Afia Sun Kim, Rex Agyemang, April Picon, Eva Ting, Christy Choi, Hannah Newman-Pan, Juliya Joseph, and of course Ignacio Aberdeen.

In a very powerful way, God was drawing us all together. We grew in life and ministry, supporting one another as companions in a creative and risk-taking endeavor of establishing and then nurturing along a new seminary, seeking the well-being of our neighborhoods, supporting the future of churches in our city. We are still finding our way, growing in friendship with God and one another.

After years of dreaming, planning, and working together, Allan and I were now in different cities, recognizing the different directions and approaches we were each pursuing. We would also pick back up almost daily our old ways of speaking frequently, and of meeting whenever possible, catching up on family, politics, sports, and music, and reflecting on our faith for our times.[8]

Memorably, my friend Jerry Callaghan, who played a formative role in my life in New York, providing seasoned wisdom and prayer, got Allan and me tickets to the Knicks versus the Lakers, with Kobe Bryant (as best I recall) and Shaquille O'Neal. Floor seat tickets, to be exact. More than once during the game I was worried that Shaq was going to crash onto Allan, crushing him, and there was nothing I could have done to stop that. But rarely had I seen Allan happier!

Now settled in New York, for my fortieth birthday in 2001, Allan wrote me a letter:

---

8. I commend the work of Henri Nouwen in this whole area. For these matters elsewhere, see Hauerwas, "Friendship and Freedom."

Birds

> *We have virtually been through it all together. You have always been there for me and my family, period. And that includes when no one else has. Thanks for being there always; there are not many people in all of history that have a friend as loyal as you. I can't wait to see what God does in you, with you, and through you during the next forty years!*

This was the same Allan who had hung out with me in high school youth group and who'd encouraged me in ministry. He was always there, always encouraging me to keep going, pursuing our mutual commitment to ministry in the cities to which God had called us.

Looking back is important. Henri Nouwen's *Gracias: A Latin American Journal* is a moving meditation on his personal ministry journey at an important time in his life. It also became instructive to me. As one seeks to clarify one's calling (Nouwen writes), it can be hard to see how God is at work in an in-between time. But by looking back, he could see how God had been connecting the threads of his ministry and vocation.[9] I found this to be true in my life, too.

I could not have ever planned or imagined what was going to take place in New York and the people who would shape my life, the opportunity to work together for the Gospel. As in Sandtown, it was "all the Spirit," Pastor Adebisi Oyesile reminded me.

In the global city of New York with a global dimension to church life, I had to unlearn what I thought I knew about cities and ministry from Baltimore in order to be present to what God was doing in a different city and ecclesial reality. As we find in the book of Jeremiah, the prophet calls the Lord's people to be present to the city where they have been moved by God. Here they are called to love the streets, people, and life where they are set. For only in the peace of the city where they dwell will they find their peace, well-being for their families and future. Bloom where you are planted, as the saying goes!

But in a way, Sandtown made City Seminary possible. I can now see how everything we experienced in Sandtown, what I learned from and with Allan, was critical in forming City Seminary of New York. I learned that community formation is about building up the gifts of others, being willing and able to persevere and learn from difficult situations and circumstances, focusing on spirituality, celebrating life, laughing as you go, drawing strength from the community. How to be open to what can happen!

9. See Nouwen, *Gracias!*

Sharing the Crust

Although I am all in as a Yankees pinstripes person (thank you Mariano Rivera and teammates!) in my heart I still cheer for the Birds of Baltimore. Let's go, O's!

Three

Three words tell the story of New Song, of Allan. *Keep at it.*

On Monday morning in Sandtown, more than 140 children arrive at New Song Academy and Learning Center. Mr. Kelley, Sean, Jane, and Susan meet them at the entrance, welcoming each student by name. They move into well-designed small classrooms in a beautiful new school and community center, built on a once vacant lot. High school, then college are next stops. All the while, teachers who are agents of hope, really ministers of hope, who accompany students on their life journey, are making the school a home base for life. The staff are largely parents and everyday people from the neighborhood.

With a staff also from the neighborhood, the health center on Fulton Avenue is open and serves the neighborhood, providing primary care. Antoine Bennett and Patty Prasado-Rao labor together to strengthen the overall work of Habitat and New Song. Jenny is a summer intern, and Jessica is working at the Learning Center preschool. Nina Anderson is the director of EDEN Jobs, meeting daily with her neighbors to help them find employment, maintain it, and develop their gifts. Thurman Williams is pastoring, following Steve and Mary Smallman, Wy and Shirley Plummer. And a neighborhood business has opened called Gerry's Goods, named for Gerry Palmer who is in his store everyday.

Saturday is for house dedications, sometimes two or three a month, complete with churches, neighbors, staff, the gift of a Bible, the house keys, and joyous singing of "This Little Light" on the street. This is the fruit of what LaVerne, Allan, Ike, Gary, Orlando, Charles, Mike, and others are doing to mobilize thousands of people a year to join in eliminating vacant housing in Sandtown through community home ownership. Block by block, house by house, abandoned houses are being replaced by homes of beauty.

Sharing the Crust

And then on Sunday, a faith community gathers, raising their arms in joyful praise to God, testifying, and hearing the Word. Come Monday, the work begins again, with thousands of little things being done each day to support one another, a pattern of one day and six days, a dynamic of liturgy and justice to structure our life.[1] The whole neighborhood, at least the fifteen blocks where we live and focus, feels like a joyous construction site and revival service at the same time. The atmosphere is different.

In this second decade of New Song, New Song is living its purpose, expressing "love, not in word or speech, but in truth and action," as we read in 1 John 3:18. The combined New Song staff has now doubled to almost one hundred from where it stood after the first ten years. They are each doing their work, what they are called to do.

New Song was encouraged by involvement in John Perkins's nationwide Christian Community Development Association (CCDA). Sandtown was finding not merely technical knowledge but transformational knowledge upon which people could draw to change their lives, neighborhood, and city.[2] Paul Stoller, an anthropologist of great insight, finds that such community-based expertise and knowledge, gained through experience, is critical not just for local well-being, but also for the world that we all inhabit.[3] It is not so much a linear journey as a way of life, of practices of singing, building, laughing, praying, and being together.[4]

"We go on," Daniel Berrigan wrote in his autobiography, *To Dwell in Peace*. "It is, oftener than not, a contest of sheer endurance. The same actions stretch ahead, wearying and energizing at once. No matter: keep at it."[5]

Keep at it.

With these three words, "Keep at it," Allan would always sign off a conversation, end a sermon, conclude an email. "Keep at it" are words of moral and spiritual responsibility. They reflect a commitment, an obligation Allan held about building housing and community in Sandtown, about responding to hardship, about the "sheer endurance" that a life committed to peace and social justice required—an obligation wearying and energizing at the same time.

1. Wolterstorff, *Until Justice and Peace Embrace*; *Hearing the Call*; and *Justice*.
2. Hope and Timmel, *Training for Transformation*, 14.
3. Stoller, *Adventures in Blogging*.
4. Lederach and Lederach, *When Blood and Bones Cry Out*.
5. Berrigan, *To Dwell in Peace*, 304.

Three

Keeping at it is also the way of loving kindness or *hesed*, as the Hebrew Scriptures describe, keeping faith and truth in relationship. Allan, New Song keeping at it, practicing loving kindness, week by week.

But Allan is not just "keeping at it": he is "abiding." In the Gospel of John, "abiding" speaks of home, an image of staying, putting down deep roots, being a part of something life-giving, even eternal, and of bearing fruit.[6] Not just any fruit, but fruit that is joy, peace, gentleness, and hope. By keeping at it, his life in the chair and in Sandtown were a witness of love to God and life in God.

But even for Allan, who enjoyed making to-do lists in his journal and on scraps of paper, the now unending scope of things could be overwhelming. Each vacant house required negotiation with a private landlord, state agencies, or different branches of city government. There was also the personal involvement with each family, which kept expanding, block by block.

And then there were all the different aspects of New Song for which others looked to him, relationships still at the center of everything. He continued to do the little and necessary things each day that made community work, "the drudgery of the kingdom" as he called it. But now it all seemed to be compounding, overwhelming his ability to stay on top of things.

Funding was not easy, and the work grew more complex with each component of the model that the group added. A decision was made to close the health center. And at one point, with funds depleted and Allan's health at issue, Habitat had to shut down operations for several months. As Allan wrote in his journal on February 2, 2002, sentiments similar to what he would write and share countless times, the "money [was] not flowing in as it needs to." He went on. "I have prayed intensely about all of this, asking God what's up and begging for his mercy. I do not doubt his sovereignty, but I do not know what his plan is for New Song at this point. But I trust him."

And then in 2007, seemingly "out of nowhere," but thanks to deep friendship, New Song and Sandtown Habitat received a transformational multi-year gift in memory of Skip Viragh. Skip, an immensely successful business leader who died of pancreatic cancer, had directed that the bulk of his estate be used to "give back" and to "help others." Guided by his life and faith, his family saw New Song and Sandtown Habitat as one way to honor those wishes.

---

6. For a larger study that captures something of the riches of abiding in Scripture, see Quash, *Abiding*. See also Ford, *Gospel of John*, 292.

Now, for the first time ever in New Song's history, the core work of New Song is fully funded, and all debts incurred for the new center are cleared.

When he received news of the gift in honor of Skip, Allan wrote of how he called Susan, sharing tears of both relief and gratitude. The legacy and faith of Skip Viragh, and his family, were now also part of Sandtown.

With his body acutely susceptible to overheating, Allan was at this point regularly suffering from migraine headaches, kidney problems, and pressure sores, among the many complications of being a quadriplegic. Having a critical health condition, as Allan did, and continuing to suffer so much pain made him particularly susceptible to "anxiety" (a word he used). In light of the needs of his neighbors, knowing he was dependent upon hospitals and air conditioning to keep on living as a quadriplegic made him uneasy.[7]

"The pain of the world and life here continues to weigh on me every second," Allan recorded in his journal as a summary of where he was emotionally and spiritually.

What made Allan be Allan in the neighborhood was his love and care for each person, his tears over each loss and injustice. He loved Sandtown and regularly thanked his neighbors for what he called "the privilege of being in the community."

Certain losses hurt more, and even haunted him; Allan never stopped mourning Rodney, Frank's brother, who in 1993 had been found dead in a basement from a gunshot, and Wyvetra Gray, who died in 1998; both had died far too early. And not every Sandtown Habitat homeowner stayed in their home; each story that did not work out was painfully crushing to Allan. He—and we—could have done better, done more, he would say. We should stay with the pain and hurt, Allan believed.

In these winter years, depending on the day—and even the time of day—when you spoke with him, Allan believed either that his work with New Song was bringing real healing to the neighborhood, or that he was coming up so short that he was in despair. Whatever the full picture was, by coming to terms with "failure," Allan was drawing closer to the heart of Christ and the cross.

---

7. Allan often turned to a *Reformed Journal* article and later Inter Varsity Fellowship booklet called *The Salvation of Zachary Baumkletter*, a parable about an individual who gave up everything to share with others, by George I. Mavrodes. For a theological discussion on how we might respond to the needs around us, see Brackley, "Downward Mobility."

Three

After lamenting his "failure," Allan wrote in his journal on February 17, 2002, that "the little things are in fact monumental." For Allan, the list of "little things" included music recitals performed by neighborhood kids, celebrating birthdays, a good meal in Little Italy, trips with Susan to places like Kent Island and Charlottesville, and a neighbor building a ramp for Allan to come into his home. They were "little things" of great beauty and community.

A connection that Allan did not know about was that Dorothy Day had looked to Saint Thérèse as a spiritual guide and even wrote a book about her life.[8] Just as Thérèse of Lisieux had emphasized "the little way" of caring for those around us with love, Day followed this with her emphasis on everyday actions of love shared with those in need.

From our first days, this was Allan's story, his own way of being, ordinary and daily acts of friendship and love. He was connected by prayer and love to Thérèse of Lisieux and Dorothy Day, part of a cloud of witnesses showing him the way in neighborhood ministry, and in his search for wholeness. In little ways, to the guys on the corner he talked with every day, to the routines of Habitat, and with his neighbors on Stricker Street, Allan kept turning the world just a bit more to the friendship and love of God, and one another, that we all seek.

In his journal on August 23, 2003, Allan begins by citing a section from Howard Thurman's *The Centering Moment*:

> *We recall with gratitude the dreams of earlier years, of the enthusiasm with which we looked out upon the world as we began our adventure, either as little children, or as adolescents, or as middle-aged or older persons—all of the dreams that have comforted and sustained us as we have passed through, or as we are passing through, the vicissitudes of life which sometimes seem to offer too much that casts down and depresses and so little that uplifts and inspires.*

Then follows Allan's reflection on Howard Thurman's words, acknowledging the critical perspective he always had on his own efforts, alongside an appreciation of a bigger picture:

> *I too often wonder what I have done, what am I doing, and feel quite small and insignificant to those who I see engaged and changing the world, and so as I read this several times one late night and thought about what I dreamed and what is the reality. Upon reflecting, I realized that my dreams were quite precisely of my present reality.*

---

8. Loughery and Randolph, *Dorothy Day*, 288–89.

> *Where else would I be? Again, if I could be anywhere with anyone doing anything, it would be right here right now with Susan and Jen and Jess doing what God has created me to, what he has "gifted" me to do, the works he has created in advance for me to walk in with joy.*

The church belongs on the corner, places like where Calhoun, Baker, and Stricker meet, Allan thought, with the guys. The church is to be a "field hospital," an image elevated by Pope Francis, as a community of presence and healing. As Allan reflected in his journal on July 10, 2007 on a New Song worship service, he wrote: "I looked around and saw a group of absolutely 'messed up' folks—me with my precarious health issues . . . [others] with depression, drug addiction, others with poverty, ex-offenders . . . We're a mess, and yet we're all here, struggling together in our seeking after God and his kingdom."

As part of this journal entry on March 8, 2008, Allan reflected on how he understood the meaning of church life in Sandtown:

> *The testimony time this morning gave reason for our being here, for the entire 20 years of struggle. What a picture of the kingdom, of the church and what it should be! I am so truly humbled that God would allow me such privilege to be in the place of such great blessing and to hear and experience the testimonies of great saints of his and to enter into their world and their pain and struggle as well as their joys and hopes. They are my, our, extended family, and it is an eternal family.*
>
> *I have so much to be thankful for that I could indeed type until daylight. The love of God ignites my life!*

A few weeks later, on August 31, 2008, Allan journaled about how, as he put it, "great saints" like Nina, Mamie, Antoine, Ryan, Lillian, "and others blessed and sustained" him. His friend Mark Lange, who had recently moved to the neighborhood with his wife Betty, was of great help to Allan.

Allan loved New Song and the community that God had brought together from Sandtown. He could see it, name what it means to be church.

There is Nina "raising her arms to God as she worships," no matter what she faces. Then there's Mamie, who "has experienced so much pain and struggle in her life that I have no idea how she keeps going, yet she is always grateful and always thankful to God and loving others as she did this morning when she hugged me and hugged and encouraged Monira; she is blessed by God and surely has great reward ahead"; and there's Antoine

Three

"who did his time on the streets and in prison and survived only to grow into a leader who cries over the pain here but rejoices over every blessing." Then there's Ryan, "a Baltimore City policeman [who] lives here and loves the kids of the neighborhood, opening his home to them and serving them in myriad ways every single day." And Lillian who, whatever her hardships, is "thankful to God and keeps reaching out to love others as she did Clarence's mom this morning on her block whose only son, age twenty-three, was shot dead earlier this week at Stricker and Laurens."

Allan continued:

> This list goes on and on: moms raising kids on their own, struggling to make ends meet and to keep their kids from the streets, with many having lost their children to the streets either from homicide or imprisonment; fathers who feel like abject failures at many levels; many people dealing with mental or physical pain. New Song is comprised of the poor, the oppressed, the marginalized, the outcasts, virtually all of whom love and trust God and have treasure stored up in heaven. I fit in to this group, and I am both humbled and honored to be counted among them, to be one of them. I deeply feel that I do not deserve such abundant blessing! Why has God allowed me such richness?

Indeed, love in community sustained him. The faith and friendship of Antoine strengthened him, and with so many others in the church and neighborhood, gave him an example of how to trust and follow Christ.

Yet Allan struggled immensely with his life and work, failing to see how he was making a difference, how he could go on. In response he continually turned to hear God in Scripture.

He would often type the words of the apostle Paul to the Galatians into his journal, "Let us not become weary in doing good, for at the proper time we will reap a harvest if we do not give up." Similarly, he would quote what was perhaps his favorite biblical text—1 Corinthians 15:58—which spoke of life freely lived in the resurrected Christ. "Therefore, stand firm. Let nothing move you. Always give yourself fully to the work of the Lord, because you know that your labor in the Lord is not in vain."[9]

Through his brokenness to the core, his own sense of sin, Allan was going deeper into his calling. In 2008, instead of his usual typing on a

---

9. Other key texts for Allan that appeared in journals, sermons, and notes are: Galatians 6:9, Romans 8:18, 1 Corinthians 15:58, 2 Corinthians 4:16, 2 Corinthians 11:23–29 and 12: 9–10, and Hebrews 12:1–3. The book of Job also continued to be crucial for Allan.

keyboard, Allan wrote out by hand the following words and biblical texts on the back of scratch paper. It was a slow process, but the practice was a physical way of affirming his faith:

> *On a Sunday morning in which I am weary, weak, overwhelmed and confused . . . lonely, feeling loss, carrying a heavy weight, hurting deeply for my father and family and so many in my neighborhood . . . feeling burdened by Habitat.*
>
> *Matthew 11:28–30 "Come to me, all you who are weary and burdened, and I will give you rest. Take my yoke upon you and learn from me, for I am gentle and humble in heart, and you will find rest for your souls. For my yoke is easy and my burden is light."*
>
> *2 Cor. 12:9–10 "My grace is sufficient for you, for my power is made perfect in weakness." "Therefore, I will boast all the more gladly about my weaknesses, so that Christ's power may rest on me. That is why, for Christ's sake, I delight in weaknesses, in insults, in hardships, in persecutions, in difficulties. For when I am weak, then I am strong."*
>
> *Phil. 4:4–7 "Rejoice in the Lord always. I will say it again: Rejoice! Let your gentleness be evident to all. The Lord is near. Do not be anxious about anything, but in every situation, by prayer and petition, with thanksgiving, present your requests to God. And the peace of God, which transcends all understanding, will guard your hearts and your minds in Christ Jesus."*
>
> *This word brings perspective, comfort, peace, rejoicing and worship, yet I remain overwhelmed with responsibilities and more than I can accomplish, even if I could work like I once did—and so I pray for wisdom that God would make clear the path and work the circumstances as they should be.*

Continuing his practice of thinking and praying through his journal, on June 22, 2009, Allan wrote:

> *I am weary, and I consider often that my remaining days are likely few, but even these things I consider part of the immense blessing of my life. Daily life is joyful, from reading the paper and drinking coffee, doing the Jumble and Sudoku, following the Orioles and getting on Mark as the Yankees lose, playing ball with Cashmere, and enjoying work as God has provided Mike at the right time and funding is abundant. I enjoy reflecting on our 20+ years here and seeing the*

Three

> *fruit continue to unfold day by day, and I feel very much a part of the extended family here that I love and who loves me.*

As Allan's body declined, his own suffering moved him to prayer.

> *I don't know what's ahead, I don't know what our impact has been, but I remain fully committed to the principles of fully expending myself on behalf of the kingdom and to the model developed by [John] Perkins, loving God and loving my neighbors in a spirit of repentance and servanthood. I pray that my life would be a picture of "knowing our best songs and singing them with my life." I pray that my life would reflect calm in the midst of the raging storm, of righteous anger and lamentation but peace and joy and perseverance even so.*

This prayer mirrors the first entry Allan wrote in his journal in 1978, "Don't know exactly what lies ahead, but to know that each day spent with you will be an adventure causes me to eagerly anticipate each tomorrow. My main concern, O Lord, is that I would set aside, completely give up, myself and my abilities so totally as to have your work done in your way." Allan was living this prayer.

As Allan reflected on what he knew were his remaining days, he drew strength from friends Charles Marsh and John Perkins and their words in *Welcoming Justice: God's Movement Toward Beloved Community*.

> *January 16, 2010*
>
> *I talked with Antoine yesterday, expressing my lament, tears and anger, all of which he shares ("I cry every day, AT."), but he stated his glass-half-full convictions as he consistently does as to why we should continue onward with great hope. In* Welcoming Justice: God's Movement Toward Beloved Community *by Charles Marsh and John Perkins, Marsh states:*
>
>> *Most of my students who have left the faith have left not because they read Kant's critique of the ontological and cosmological arguments for the existence of God, but because they have listened to Christians in hope of hearing beautiful songs and have instead heard something thin and shrill. But the church has beautiful songs to sing. Fannie Lou Hamer and John Perkins know our best songs and have sung them with their lives. And when we listen closely, we can hear the songs of other men and women who work day in and day out in inauspicious places to bring healing to the broken and blistered world. They are carried and strengthened and nourished by deep spiritual waters.*

Near the end of his life, Daniel Berrigan gave a message to peacemakers around the theme of perseverance. "You have no right to tie yourself in knots because you want to know the outcome of what you are doing. Don't, no, no. Let it go. Let it go into history. Let it go into Christ. Let it into generations. Let it go into the children. Play it and pray it well."[10]

I can hear Allan saying, *Amen*! Rebuilding Sandtown. Living in Sandtown. Brimming with hope for his neighbors, for one another. Keeping at it. I can see how Sandtown and Allan played it and prayed it well.

And you know what else I can see? A community of ragtag and bobtail, moving the same pile of dirt, laughing, crying, trying to do too much, a bit of fussing, a few choice words, eating fried cheese sticks at Bennigan's in the Inner Harbor, and giving thanks to God.

New Song being its best, most true self. Keeping at it!

---

10. McElwee, "Berrigan's Message to Peacemakers."

Fire

Word travels fast in the neighborhood.

Allan was at the Sandtown Habitat office on Fulton Avenue when word reached him. The building is an arrangement of desks, a basement loading dock, and two floors of warehouse space filled to the brim with construction supplies, kitchen sets, power tools, and hard hats, the logistics base for converting shells of bricks into homes of beauty.

Thousands of people had now come to know this corner of Fulton and Laurens as a place to meet week after week, getting work assignments to build homes in the neighborhood, but also finding a way to ensure that every wall of separation, from walls of the imagination to concrete highways, would begin to crumble. Fulton was a community center, a base of operations for building up the neighborhood.

When word reached him, Allan left immediately, pressing his electric wheelchair forward as fast it would go, aware of every curb cut or not, every crevice of the worn asphalt streets, every house between Fulton and Stricker, a trip taken thousands of times. East two blocks on Laurens Street, past Fox's Liquor store and Morton's Funeral Home, and then at the coordinates of the basketball courts and the asphalt lot of Gilmor Elementary, around the corner and up Stricker.

Arriving at the red brick row house on Stricker, he sees the front door is knocked down from a raid, and the police are now out front. Because no one was home. Because it was the wrong house. Because the house that was raided was Allan and Susan's home.

For over twenty-five years, "Allan and Susan's" had been a center of community. Jenny and Jessica's place, daughters now grown. Fitt and Gary, family too. Ky'Asia, of course. Two cats. A place for a meal, an ear to bend, a prayer to offer, a basketball game to review, a Ravens or Orioles win to celebrate. Everyone in the neighborhood knew that. Except the police, it seems.

It isn't the door that matters. Well, the broken new door does matter, but Orlando and Gary are there and will put it back on. What matters is the sum of indignities, the accruing of injustices, the cosmic wrong of it all for the neighborhood. What matters is what the broken door unmasks.

Allan's gift of prophetic conscience is a fire in his bones. As the scholar of the Hebrew prophets, Abraham Heschel, explained, it is not just what the prophets said, but God's passion living through them.[1] As they are in relationship to God, for the prophets there is first the pain, then the anger, the suffering with, followed by the body prophesying. There is a fire in their bones, like in Jeremiah, and now that fire, that passion, is flowing out of Allan. There is a commitment in his life to see differently like Daniel, Amos, Micah, Ezekiel, Isaiah.

Looking at the police, Allan clears his throat and begins to raise his voice, at least as much as he can because the muscles that normally work to expand a person's lungs are weakened in his body by paralysis.

Later, he wrote the following about the incident:

> *The head detective was extremely polite and apologetic, said to me, "So what you are saying is that there should be no police force?" I told him there must be legalization of drugs, that in the meantime the residents and police are virtual enemies with the police causing pain and hardship. He asked me if I was advocating for legalization and I told him yes.*

No police force? Allan left his answer hanging in the air, but he knew what he thought.[2] He was thinking not just about the police, but about imagining a different way of seeing how communities can and should work. Allan was rejecting justifications for violence, for keeping Sandtown down.

Legalization of drugs? The terms "legalization" and "decriminalization" of drugs are often used interchangeably, but either way, for Allan drugs were a symptom and not the cause of trouble. Instead, the whole situation was a public health crisis, driven by an economy that had written off the neighborhood, by a lack of belonging in our world. Countless lives had been destroyed by addictions, especially to heroin, Baltimore's historic drug of choice. And as a consequence, nearly Allan's life too.

---

1. Heschel, *Prophets*. See Barnes's reading of Heschel in his *Waiting on Grace*, 140–72.

2. For a historical argument on why Allan's concerns are linked, see Hinton, *From the War on Poverty*.

Fire

Some twenty years earlier, in the same place where Allan and the detective were now talking, two men passing through the neighborhood had forced their way inside the same Stricker Street house. With a large knife taken from the kitchen, they placed it at Allan's throat. Holding his neck so hard that Allan could hardly breathe, they took Allan around the house in search of cash and valuables. Shaking, they seemed to Allan to be desperate "addicts." Threatening Allan, they told him they could "kill him in a minute." He believed them.

As all of this was happening, with the knife still to his neck, Allan said he would pray for them. "Are you a churchman? Are you sure you will?" one of them asked in response. When they were about to leave, Allan told them that he "loved them and would definitely pray for them." Reflecting afterwards on what had happened, and the myriad of scenarios that could have unfolded, Allan wrote in his journal:

> I realized . . . in praying that Christ was treated harshly and responded in love, and I should do the same. I believe God was working in the guy who asked for prayer, who is hurting so much.

Allan knew that each addiction was a crisis of hope, a crisis that follows from an absence of stable foundations, like health, rest, hope, employment, and means of joy across many Baltimore years. The dealers too, shaking it up on the corners, were exhibiting this lack of hope and of stable foundations, seeing drug dealing as the only alternative in an economy that had long ago collapsed upon them like a falling, vacant building.

In freedom derived from God, from faith shaped by the Scriptures, Allan rejected the necessity of the way things are, from the police state to the prison system. He believed them to be unjust and that therefore there should be no place for them. In this sense, Allan was a prison and police abolitionist, although he didn't use those terms.

In hope, and in community, and with all he had, Allan had worked to offer an alternative to mass incarceration and the prison system by the witness of the church to the gospel. Everything New Song was trying to do was this alternative, joined by naming how the systems, the powers of death were destroying young lives, families, and the neighborhood.[3] Sandtown, Baltimore, didn't need more jail cells and an entrenched penal system, but jobs and life-giving ways, and a greater sense of community.

---

3. See Coates, "Black Family."

Sharing the Crust

After decades in Sandtown, Allan didn't see the police, the prisons, the entire system in Baltimore as being reformable. Cosmetic changes would last only for a moment. Without changes that went deep, to the underlying direction of things, without something different in its place, Allan thought (and repeatedly shared with all who would listen), Sandtown, and West Baltimore more broadly, would continue to be "volatile," a "powder keg" that could detonate at any moment, for too many layers of pain and too many decades of scars had accrued there.

It could happen any time, Allan said, and then it happened, just a few years later. On the morning of April 12, 2015, a young man named Freddie Gray was arrested in the Gilmor Homes just off North Mount Street. Following interaction with police, Gray was left with injuries to his spinal column, and he died a short time later. On the day of his funeral, the city erupted in fury and flames, its pain accumulated over decades and lifetimes turned to protest. The governor placed the National Guard on the streets of Sandtown and across the city.

Yes, Allan saw death was everywhere, but its power was defeated on the cross and in the resurrection. Therefore, the answer to the struggles of the neighborhood was seeing Sandtown differently, "regarding no one from a human [worldly] point of view" but instead seeing all "in Christ" (2 Corinthians 5:16, 17). To live in Christ in the neighborhood, in the way of the cross, in the power and hope of the resurrection: this is what mattered to Allan, and how he sought to approach everything.[4]

But on the streets of Sandtown, on that day in front of his house, in the most evangelical of moments, instead of despair and giving up, Allan gave witness to a different way—the way of living with and supporting one another, the way of abounding in tenderness, love, and mercy, of coming to a place of belonging beyond fear, the way of what the biblical writers called true shalom and peace. He sought the way of simple caring, of seeing, hearing, and listening. In a phrase from Dorothy Day, Allan believed in the transformative power of love in community. This is what God wanted for Sandtown, for Baltimore, thought Allan.

Allan placed the events of the day in his journal and then concluded no one would be held accountable for what happened to his door and his house that day. Accountability had never happened before, so why now? The police, wrote Allan, were "part of the oppressive institution currently in place, which I think includes the entire criminal justice system."

---

4. Stringfellow, *Instead of Death*, 57.

Fire

These are the final words Allan would place in his journal.

Music

Ike was calling me on a Saturday morning.

Mamie, he has just learned, has been diagnosed with inoperable cancer. I immediately picture Mamie on the front stoop of North Mount Street, her life interwoven with that of others, her care, struggle, our friendship, our prayers, plates of food, and words all shared. I can picture Ike handing her the keys to her new Habitat home on Fulton Avenue, a house he helped to build in an organization he helped to found. I can hear the sadness in Ike's voice.

With plans for Mamie to come home from the hospital in a few days, we agree that I will come and see her then. And, by the way, Ike asks as our conversation is ending, do I know why Allan is in the hospital?

Whenever Allan went to the hospital, whether for an increasingly regular kidney procedure or anything else, he would always let me know in advance so that I could pray for him. And when he returned home, he would call to let me know that he had made it, then go to bed and begin the days of recovery that his body required. Ike's question makes me realize Allan and I haven't spoken in some days.

For the past few years, Allan and I have spoken often about his dying, the way of the cross he had taken up with his life, his living hope in the resurrection of Christ, the meaning of his work in Sandtown.

We had always read and discussed together ideas that circulated about Scripture, the city, community development, and neighborhoods, passing books and articles back and forth between us. At Allan's request, I had passed along to him Carlos Eire's *A Very Brief History of Eternity* and German theologian Jürgen Moltmann's *In the End—The Beginning*,[1] important writing on faith and the future of our lives.

---

1. Eire, *Very Brief History*, and Moltmann, *In the End*.

MUSIC

But now above all else, I'd noticed that Allan was reading more Scripture, deepening his life of prayer, shutting out other things. Looking back on those last weeks and months, I now recognize that with each conversation we had, he was readying himself for his death. And looking back at photographs from that time, I can see how much his health and his physical strength was waning.

Allan, I now learn following Ike's call, is in Mercy Hospital, and very ill. The last time we were together had been a few months earlier when I went to Baltimore to thank Allan for helping the seminary lease a new campus.

One of the first people I'd met in New York was Ken Haron, a housing developer working in Harlem. Ken not only became my teacher about housing and development in New York, but a close friend and conversation partner on all matters of faith, the city, and politics, even as we often disagreed. Working with Ken, the possibility arose of a new space across the street from our seminary storefront. When I ran the idea by Allan, he immediately urged us to move forward, convinced particularly of its importance for the growth of our work in the neighborhood.

A few days before the deadline to close on the property, the money for the deposit still outstanding, the deal was in danger of falling through. Allan called to tell me that what we needed would be coming as a gift from Sandtown. I had not expected this at all. This gift, I would eventually see, was not simply another time of finding a way to get something done, of loaves and fishes, but a parting blessing. This gift was Allan's hands placed upon my life, a passing on of the work we had done together in Christ for so much of our lives.

Now, a few months later, the lease signed, the weather warmer, I went to Baltimore to thank Allan, Ike, Antoine, LaVerne, Thurman, Mike, Patty, and others at New Song who had helped to make our new campus possible. We shared a meal and conversation outside at an Inner Harbor restaurant, enjoying the wide-open public space at the heart of Baltimore. It was fitting, as this is where we always turned as the place to be for an important meal and any needed walk around the city.

After lunch, Allan took me back to the train station. As I got ready to leave his van, we shared a prayer, I told him how much I loved him, thanking him not just for the gift, but for everything. We could both well recall the countless times we had spent together, and perhaps felt somehow that this was to be the last time. Slowly, reluctantly, we parted company and I caught my train back to New York.

It was indeed the last time I saw Allan.

A few days after Ike called me to say that Mamie was sick, on May 30, 2010 she passed into the arms of the Lord. I mourned for Ike. But I also knew, as we read in the Psalms, "Precious in the sight of the Lord, Is the death of his faithful ones" (Psalm 116:15). With plans to travel to Baltimore for Mamie's funeral, I decided to wait and see Allan then.

Knowing Allan was in the hospital, I was continually checking my phone, hoping for an update from Susan, even as Rita and I sat in a small concert hall in Manhattan. For the final piece, the orchestra begins to perform Beethoven's String Quartet in C Sharp Minor, a musical composition I was hearing for the first time.

As the piece gains momentum, its movements swirling and driving, I suddenly begin to feel Allan experiencing the storms that are within the music. I find myself following him there, carried body and soul into a world of churning desolation.

I am unable to move. All I find myself doing is pleading with God that the storm and its vicious powers will pass, that Allan will travel in peace to a world of divine love. I want the music to stop. I want Allan to be free of suffering and present to a new life with God. I want his end to be a new beginning without end.

And then the musical piece ends. The storm is over.

The next morning, as I was walking our son Daniel to school, I received Susan's call that Allan had died overnight. One final time, music had connected Allan and me, our "own internal weather," to quote Teju Cole.[2] Words from 1 John could not have been more apt in that moment: "We know that we have passed from death to life because we love one another" (1 John 5:14).

Friendship was the heart of the life that God had given to the two of us. In friendship and ministry, Allan and I worked to establish communities and build ministries in Baltimore and New York that served the peace of the city, sought to bridge racial, geographical, and economic lines, lighten the burdens of our neighbors, and raised our children to be mindful of God's love and purposes for the world. We were drawn together by a dream, we passed through many fires, and we worked together as companions in Christ's mission.[3]

---

2. Cole, *Known and Strange Things*, 7. My thanks to Chris Scharen for this quotation.

3. Some of the wording here comes from the song "Pilgrim Companions" by the St. Louis Jesuits.

Music

Bruce Cockburn and his music had been uniquely life-giving in our story. It is perhaps not surprising then that Cockburn's exquisitely beautiful song "Isn't That What Friends Are For?" is where I find the words to describe the journey Allan and I had shared.:

> I've been scraping little shavings off my ration of light
> And I've formed it into a ball, and each time I pack a bit more onto it
> I make a bowl of my hands and I scoop it from its secret cache
> Under a loose board in the floor
> And I blow across it and I send it to you
> Against those moments when
> The darkness blows under your door
>
> Isn't that what friends are for?[4]

At its heart, our friendship had been sharing our "ration of light," our ability to recognize and celebrate God's presence in our journey and vocations, to see and hope in faith for one another whatever risks, challenges and new projects we undertook. To share light so we could live what is good, what is just and right, what bears fruit.

And when the darkness blew under our doors, as Cockburn's imagery puts it—and there was rarely a season or year when it did not do so with great frequency and in a multitude of ways—Allan and I found a way to send each other "little shavings off [our] ration[s] of light." The light we shared was the light of God, the light that shines in the darkness (John 1:5).

Our friendship over time lay in our ability to recognize and celebrate the light of God's presence in our journey and vocations, to share the ration of what we had so we could live what is good, what is just and right. It was to see and hope in faith for one another, whatever risks and new projects we took on. It was to say, "Yes, you can do that," to one another.

Our friendship was to help one another change, to repent, to live in love for our neighbors, to take on a different calling in life.[5] And this is why genuine, true friendship helps us to face our own blind spots, to grow in self-knowledge and honesty.[6] There was immense trust, respect, and shared commitment at the foundation of our history. We were on a pilgrimage together, going in the same direction.

---

4. Bruce Cockburn, "Isn't That What Friends Are For?"

5. For more on the theological dynamics of friendship, see Parsons, "Friendship for Others."

6. Wadell, *Friendship and the Moral Life*, 155.

Yet Allan and I were not carbon copies of one another. It wasn't just that we disagreed over commas and sports—which we did! Our genuinely different points of view, histories, and personalities were part of our uniqueness, without which, we often said, we would not have accomplished much of what we did in Sandtown.

From reading Allan's journals, given to me by Susan after his death, I now know that he often felt I let him down, mishandled a meeting or an activity or a problem in the church, and to his mind, failed to support his vocation. At least at the moments he wrote in his journals he was less than pleased with my efforts as a pastor, friend, and colleague. Ouch!

Much of what he wrote (when I could place the issue and setting to which he was referring) was right about me, and often painfully so. I am embarrassed just thinking about it, young and immature, starting out in life, in pastoral ministry. But at other times I believe that what Allan wrote was actually not accurate and that it did not show a willingness to consider other viewpoints or ways of working.

I wondered: What underlay Allan's pattern of frustration? From where did his less than beautiful shortness with me, and others closest to him, come? Was it the suffering of his critical injury? The physical setbacks in his life? The mechanisms of defense when he felt that perhaps his calling and purpose were being blocked? His need for control, intensified through his life in the chair? Was it his singular passion for the work he was doing, a drive that overrode his perspective and the cares of others closest to him? Only Allan knows what it was like for him to be a quadriplegic, and the ways it affected every aspect of his body, heart, and soul. Try as I might, and listen as I did, I can only understand some of it. We can't know everything about others, or even ourselves. Only God knows us fully.

It is true that upon first reading these entries after Allan's death, I found myself again experiencing wounds from my pastoral work in Sandtown. Alienation, I know, is part of the human condition. But in those moments, I had to recognize again what I had learned from Sister Grace, that Christ's suffering and resurrection remains a part of my own life, and there is always a grace in holding this.

Community life, and friendship in community, is exceedingly difficult, but it is all we have. Philip Berrigan and Elizabeth McAlister knew this too, and wrote about it in *The Time's Discipline*. There, they considered family and community life in the Catholic Worker Jonah House, with its vocation of peacemaking against nuclear weapons, and recalled conflicts, disappointments, differences, failures, suffering, ego, and triviality.[7]

Each of us is graced and flawed, as are our communities, which is why ministry is never experienced as an ideal. As we found, something like New Song can move and bless, but such a close setting can also prompt unhealed wounds to re-emerge, often more painfully than the first time. When deep change cuts too close to the bone (or our wounds), our defenses can go up. And when things do not turn out the way we hope, when fears overtake us, when our internal dreams are not fulfilled, and when people let us down, we often either withdraw or hurt one another.

The early forms and thinking about Christian faith emphasized a different type of community and friendship, that of welcoming one another across our experiences of alienation. A common life, and friendships, that are not closed in on itself, that is not competitive with one another. A very difficult challenge, to be sure.

This is why, in the New Testament letters of St. Paul, the life of a Christian community requires ongoing effort and work, renewal, and change. When St. Paul writes in Ephesians 4 about Christ, grace, and community, he also emphasizes the relational practices, dispositions, and habits of patience, humility, bearing with one another in love, confession, mutual forgiveness, love, and truth *together*. This suggests that he knows that at some level all relationships fail and need repair.[8]

At the root of congregational life, friendship, and every family relationship, at the root of our public life and our institutions, is the need to learn to forgive and be forgiven, to recognize our own faults and brokenness, our need for healing and for friendship. This is the way of Christ, who forgave us while we were yet sinners.

Even as Allan and I were two broken people, and could be a real pain to one another, we also lived reconciled lives over any differences we may have had, the pieces of our story taken up in grace. Hurt did not have the final word in our friendship.[9] Love does! And love, which is at the heart of friendship, outlasts death. This is the sanctification of friendship, of our friendship.

Allan did not want to be called a hero, certainly not a saint. In Allan's mind, his actions, even as a quadriplegic, were not extreme, special,

---

7. Berrigan and McAlister, *Time's Discipline*.
8. This discussion owes much to Stephen E. Fowl, *Ephesians*.
9. Wadell, *Becoming Friends*.

or altruistic. Instead, Allan just saw himself trying to love his neighbor, living out a basic Christian faith and responsibility with Susan, LaVerne, his family, and neighbors. Allan had sought an intellectual, and spiritual, assessment of his time and moment, and then lived with responsibility and grace, as best he could. We could all do something like this, he said!

But he, and Mamie and so many others in Sandtown, are among the prophets, witnesses, and saints we need. "Saints," observes Brendan Walsh, "are human beings we celebrate for their uniqueness, for their gifts—good and bad—and for their ability to help us understand both suffering and joy."[10] If Allan left behind "the chair," it is not that he is now "more like us," but that we are invited to be more like him in his vulnerability and openness to the heart of God. Like Mamie in her care and life for others. In their friendship.

If I were to paint Allan and Mamie, I would paint them as the saints they are, with iridescent halos of gold—and black Adidas shoes for Allan. They would be in the neighborhood, where with their lives, they have given witness to Christ in this time and a particular place, challenging and encouraging our fidelity to the gospel in our times and in our places.

Why not a feast day to remember Allan and Mamie, and others who have gone before us in the neighborhood? To remember their friendship, gentleness, toughness, and faith, to look at our own callings, the choices we make? After all, a banquet is how Jesus described the reign of God, and it was with a meal, on the road to Emmaus, that the resurrected Christ shared himself with the disciples.

In this spirit, once a year let there be hot dogs, hamburgers, and iced tea, healthier food too, and of course Sonia's mac and cheese. Let there be snowballs from the block, and a DJ playing the latest music and more, perhaps some Bruce Cockburn, the latest from U2, and some from the Electric Slide for remembering and dancing. And of course, let there also be garden tools, paint brushes, and hammers for all to remind us of the work we have shared and the work still to be done.

In a wonderful remembrance of Allan written by the reporter Jason DeParle for the annual year-end issue of the *New York Times Magazine* on "The Lives They Lived," he wrote, "There are programs that have built more dwellings . . . but few have built closer bonds."[11] And in an irony not to

---

10. Walsh and Bickham, *Long Loneliness in Baltimore*.
11. DeParle, "Wheelchair Missionary," 30–31.

be missed, George Steinbrenner, the late owner of the Yankees, graced the cover in the issue which Allan's story appeared. Thank you, God!

I know the future is more than I can imagine (1 Corinthians 2:9), but I picture Mamie and Allan, welcomed into the embrace of God. They are at a banquet, singing, laughing, and dancing together without end. They are at a "festival of friends,"[12] to recall the words of Bruce Cockburn, always remembering the gift we were given. The friendship of God that they experienced together in Sandtown, but now experience in all its fullness. The Spirit is in their dance!

"To Sandtown!" Mamie and Allan offer in a toast, their glasses clinking. And then they continue dancing—to the music of new creation, a new song—with the risen Son, the heart of all of creation.

---

12. Bruce Cockburn, "Festival of Friends."

Paths

Allan's funeral service was at New Shiloh Baptist Church, and the last time most of us had been at New Shiloh was with President Jimmy and Rosalynn Carter, a celebration of the rebuilding of Sandtown some twenty years earlier. Now as I look around the sanctuary, I can see Rev. Harold Carter Sr. from New Shiloh with Rev. Vaughn from Sharon Baptist in Sandtown at the front, and then the rows of the church filling in with Black and white, urban and suburban, doctors and drug dealers—the beloved community over a thousand strong. God had given us a story that was possible only with God.

Earlier in the day, Frank and I had met on Stricker Street before going over to the service. It had been nearly twenty-five years since Frank had leaned out his window on North Calhoun Street and introduced himself. Before the service, Frank had wanted to get something to eat, so we walked to a corner store in the neighborhood that sells mostly sodas, snacks, and cigarettes from behind thick plexiglass.

Sometimes Allan wondered whether Frank might be an angel that God had placed among us. Maybe this is one reason why Allan always shared with Frank whatever he had. If Frank is an angel, then he certainly watched over Allan, over us, and over the neighborhood, holding us to our truest calling. Maybe that is also a reason why, after Allan died, Susan gave Frank his jacket.

As we walked, taking a small shortcut path across a matted corner lot of dirt and stone paths, Frank launched an unprompted, improvised liturgy.

"There is Mr. Allan," Frank pointed out as we saw community gardens on the corners.

"There is Allan, too," we said as we passed blocks of beautifully rebuilt homes.

Walking past New Song Center, once a vacant lot, we see a school building that has risen and changed the futures of a generation. If the past horizons were limited, today when its children talked about their futures, they imagined themselves as doctors, lawyers, and ministers. They could see a different future for themselves.

"There is Allan," Frank and I proclaimed.

As Frank and I continue our walk on the sidewalks and paths of Sandtown, paths that I had traveled countless times, often with Allan, I recall Patti Smith and her song, "Paths that Cross."

To greet the arrival of the New Year and her birthday, Patti Smith often played a series of shows in New York at the Bowery Ballroom. Each year I would purchase two tickets, but as Allan's strength greatly diminished over the years, so did his plans for joining me at a show.

"Paths that Cross" has these beautiful lines: "On that day / Filled with grace, Paths that cross, will cross again."[1] Here on this path where Frank and I walk, that Allan and I traveled with others, this hallowed sacred earth of West Baltimore, "paths that cross will cross again." The paths that will cross again are not just friendships, but a whole pastoral and communal experience we shared together in Sandtown.

Like holy water splashed upon the neighborhood, there is sacramental blessing upon the labor of so many hands, upon the path Frank and I walk, upon the patch of earth called Sandtown, upon the city as part of God's creation. And in this place, in Sandtown, we find a sign of the gospel.

"There is a new world, the old order has gone," St. Paul describes, "and a new order has already begun" (2 Corinthians 5:17; Luke 1:46–55). We had watched the world in which we lived change before our eyes, changing in and through Christ:

> Nearly 350 families became homeowners, living in a beautiful and healthy environment, and passing along their assets to their families.
>
> Because of the years the health center was open, people lived longer, and could see better health for their family and neighborhood.
>
> Through the Learning Center, the entire future environment for young people changed. Hundreds became high school graduates, and then college graduates, and doctoral students.

---

1. Patti Smith, "Paths that Cross."

By focusing on community development, hundreds of people from the neighborhood gained jobs throughout the region, and over one hundred people had employment in the neighborhood.

Guided by a vision for the earth, five community gardens had been established, planted, and maintained.

A public witness by a community of people who took responsibility.

Bridges were built so upwards of 10,000 people a year from Baltimore and around the world could come to Sandtown to share in the work, and to build new relationships. A demonstration of the common good that people desire.

A story of what it means to be church, a call to ecclesial conversion.

In summary, God has done more than we could have asked or imagined (Ephesians 3:20).

As I consider all that transpired, I recall Millard Fuller asking us if we had one dollar. After starting out with a single dollar, by today's costs, and if done in traditional ways, the value of the work we did in rebuilding—which would benefit Sandtown families for decades to come—would be in the range of nearly $100 million.

"Never doubt," goes the famous phrase attributed to the anthropologist Margaret Mead, "that a small group of thoughtful committed individuals can change the world; indeed, it's the only thing that ever has." As we learn from Jesus, "Where two or three are gathered . . ."

Given the scope and scale of our work, is there more we can do to assess the impact of our effort in Sandtown? Perhaps, using the idea of Nobel Prize-winning economists Abhijit V. Banerjee and Esther Duflo,[2] we could compare what happened in Sandtown to what happened in a nearby neighborhood, one to which we had almost moved in 1986. In Sandtown, in the fifteen blocks on which we had focused, we could see the major change that new institutions and an intense investment by the people of the community and many others had wrought. In the other neighborhood, in which there was no such investment of money, materials, or community, the abandonment of infrastructure, hope, and community only increased.

It doesn't take a moonshot; we know what happens when we invest in families, neighborhoods, and cities.

---

2. See Banerjee and Duflo, *Poor Economics*.

Paths

In his final email sent to the staff at New Song, Allan included the "Oscar Romero prayer," words not likely from Romero but composed and passed along in his spirit:

> We accomplish in our lifetime only a tiny fraction of
> the magnificent enterprise that is God's work.
> Nothing we do is complete,
> which is another way of saying
> that the kingdom is beyond us.
>
> This is what we are about:
> We plant seeds that one day will grow.
> We water seeds already planted, knowing that they hold future promise.
> We lay foundations that will need further development.
> We provide yeast that produces effects beyond our capacities
>
> We are workers, not master builders
> ministers, not messiahs.
> We are prophets of a future not our own.

Time

Standing on this holy and hallowed patch of earth that is Sandtown, I should take my shoes off.

It is Advent, a late December evening in 1986, and Christmas Day is just around the corner. The time in the Christian calendar of longing, anticipation, when change is in the wind. A time when all things are unsettled, reality shaken up.

A young man named Joseph, a mother-to-be named Mary. Then angels and shepherds, no place to stay, and then the future rippling out in history from the cry of a tiny baby.[1] The very life of God—the One who created and holds the universe together—will be making a home in the neighborhood; so says John the Evangelist. The Word will arrive as a challenge to the powers, reconciling all that is broken, turning to peace. Inviting us to turn our lives in a new way of love, solely upon God's grace.

This is what Advent prepares us to encounter.

I am driving to Baltimore from Philadelphia, where I am completing seminary studies. Over my shoulder I see the faded industrial zone where stadiums will one day rise for the Baltimore Orioles and for a football team that will be called the Baltimore Ravens. Along Martin Luther King Boulevard, a traffic light's distance into the city, where men and women wash car windows for change and sometimes make a home in the center median, there is a parking lot amidst dollar-type stores and low-cost food shops. Allan is waiting there in his van.

The hour is late, so we exchange a few words sitting in Allan's van, a silent prayer held between us. Then Allan hands me a set of keys. He is helping me, believing in me, trusting me, the gift of friendship. I step out of his van, and we depart, Allan to his home at the time in rural Clarkesville.

---

1. Cockburn, "Cry of a Tiny Babe."

Time

A mile's drive or so along Baltimore streets, crossing an unfinished highway that goes nowhere, a jagged tear in the urban fabric, and I am in Sandtown, a neighborhood on Baltimore's West side. Allan had arranged for me to rent 1125 North Calhoun Street, to which the keys will open the door. A two-story brick row house, it is a single shade of dark red paint that uniformly covers the entire block, as if it were a tower building on its side. I park my car on the street around the corner.

Beneath the night sky, I walk along Winchester and Calhoun Streets, past Mount Pisgah Church on the corner, near old garages converted to stables for the Arabbers. There's also a hulking abandoned Schmidt Baking Company in the background. Perhaps an angel or two, and a shepherd at the stable.

At this moment, I experience a vision, like a photograph or painting: I see the neighborhood—its streets, blocks, and buildings—as they should be, with bricks and timbers held together rightly. I see friends that I did not know I had.

It is not my habit to receive visions, but I hold this close, even as I set it aside, receiving it not as a charge, but a picture of Christian life as God intends.

Advent surely is a time for the strange, the unexpected, for slowing things down to see what is really going on, what belongs together.[2] A time to encounter the Word, the first and last word about a new humanity, about creation restored, redeemed from the powers of death.[3] To recognize the Word at home in the neighborhood. Simply through the cry of a tiny baby.

At the end of a long day, lying quietly in my bed, I listen to street dogs rustling over the trash cans in the alley. A sign, and then a whispered prayer. I am grateful for Allan and for the providence that has guided me to Calhoun Street.

I fall asleep, dreams committed to Sandtown.

It is now thirty years almost to that day in 1986 when I first moved to Sandtown, when Allan handed me a set of keys, when I had a vision under the night sky, when I fell asleep to dogs rustling in the alley. Today it is Christmas, and I am back on the streets of Sandtown to see Ike and his family.

---

2. Paulsell, "Strange Stuff."
3. Stringfellow, *Instead of Death*.

Now I can see. A vision under a night sky thirty years earlier had turned out to be a picture of the Christian story, the world as it should be. God's Word had taken its course, and I can now see the neighborhood—its streets, blocks, and buildings—differently. Urban forms as they should be, bricks and timbers held together rightly. We have all been made friends in ways we never could have expected. I am different. God has given Sandtown its own time.

Thanks be to God!

Ike and I meet at the Freeloaders Social Club on Lorman Street, a block from where I had lived on North Mount. Everyone at the club is waiting for the Ravens game to start. Kurt, my friend from earliest days, is there, as is Jermaine, a neighbor and friend from Mount Street. Together with Ike we remember Allan, catch up on how Susan is doing in her new beginnings, LaVerne and her family, and other neighborhood news. The club members begin to reminisce with me about my days in the neighborhood, about what they saw, how I was always walking, always on the go. Nothing is missed in the neighborhood!

But the city has now become Freddie Gray's city, and Sandtown the fault line of a city's history and future. As a *Baltimore Sun* headline stated, "Neighborhoods are Crying Out."[4] At the time of Gray's death, the world outside West Baltimore was shocked by the scale of urban abandonment in the city, and in response, scores of vacant houses are being torn down, the parts sold off to a global economy. Once again, more vacant lots collect trash and teem with weeds. There is new damage to the urban fabric, more neighborhoods as archipelagos, fewer resources for tangible investment. There is also a great risk to the lives of firefighters who must deal with building collapses and fires in vacant houses.

The corners of Sandtown are now filled with people no one seems to know, and it is easier to acquire a "piece"—a handgun—in the neighborhood than it is to find a book to read. Young people are losing their lives as result. Overdose deaths are rising. Getting to a job like at a car wash can take upwards of three hours by foot and bus, and despite that effort, it is still not enough to support a family. The rates of incarceration are among the highest in the city. The infrastructure, like water and its systems, is failing. People are leaving the neighborhood and city. Meanwhile, the Western District police station has been refurbished, while the only grocery store in walking distance has been torn down and turned into a parking lot.

---

4. Broadwater and Duncan, "'Neighborhoods are Crying Out.'"

Time

To move forward, perhaps Baltimore, like South Africa after apartheid, and other nations and cities that followed, needs its own Commission on Truth and Reconciliation, which was led by Bishop Desmond Tutu. Truth and Reconciliation is a process of prayer, listening, confession, an aiming for justice in love. Certainly, such a process will be imperfect and provisional, but it is a way that could help bring everyone closer to greater honesty about history, to reconciliation in a society, to clarity that we need to stand together for the dignity of all persons.[5] Indeed, Wes Moore, the new governor of Maryland, writing with the reporter Erica Green after Freddie Gray died, suggested just such a proposal be considered, in our hearts and communities.[6]

Change has also come to New Song. It had taken decades and thousands of people and countless small activities to build New Song, a community of people and concrete liberation, but only a short time to dismantle it. Today, the gardens we planted are overgrown, and important buildings in our history are vacant. Sandtown Habitat and building weeks are no more, and with it, the ways people from all backgrounds and beliefs, in a fractious city and time, connect together in joy by working together on houses. The health center was already closed, and Gerry's Goods, a store and economic development effort, also closed. Other pieces of our story are in a different place,[7] and the losses ripple out.[8]

On the streets of the neighborhood, many wonder—"Did our life together even happen? Has God forgotten us?" We are trying to understand, to continue to do theology around our sorrows, and our hopes. The weight of what has been lost is so great because of the Love that abounded.

How did this change to New Song happen? Part of this is the brokenness and finitude of our human story. No matter how vital and right the calling and work, it is hard to maintain a prophetic institution; there is always a challenge to hold together Spirit and structure, community and institution. Social change for the common good never comes easy.

And then there was the great personal and family cost that everyone shared, the weariness of the work. As I recall the novels of Nadine Gordimer, like *My Son's Story*, about life during and after apartheid in South Africa, what keeps coming back to me is her way of revealing the human toll

---

5. Valiente, *Liberation Through Reconciliation*.
6. Moore with Green, *Five Days*, 258–59.
7. See Lanahan, *Lines Between Us*, 222–223, 283.
8. Brinig and Garnett, *Lost Classroom, Lost Community*.

a lengthy struggle takes, the complexities, the before and after that cost so many so much. And yet the struggle for justice still has to go on for housing, for dignity, for peace and justice, for the gospel.

The observation of Juan Luis Segundo is bracing: "The real sin against the Holy Spirit is refusing to recognize, with theological joy, some concrete liberation that is taking place before one's very eyes."[9] And if we do not see, do we evict one unclean spirit only to open ourselves up to be taken over by seven more? In freedom, Athol Gill reminds us, we can resist the powers by living under the Lordship of Christ, the practice of sacrificial love, and the way of the cross.[10] If forces yet divide and harm, Ched Myers in his work on the Gospel of Mark reminds us that the name of the Stronger One, Jesus, is the one who heals, redeems from the powers.[11]

Our vision as New Song was costly and demanded much. This is why community and vocation are journeys over a lifetime, requiring, as Howard Thurman identified, the "disciplines of the Spirit."[12] As the theologian Dorothee Soelle observed, it is not just the importance of beliefs and institutions, but the mysticism, the experiences of God in community that sustain, and press us.[13]

Indeed, an exemplary institution, as Rowan Williams observed about the view held by William Stringfellow, is one that knows it has "failed."[14] This is why it matters how we attend to our common life and calling, the choices we make that impact the future of our institutions. "We all pay for the benefits of a tradition-bearing community," Dean Brackley, a Jesuit priest who served in El Salvador, observed, "and sometimes the price is unjust; but we cannot eliminate all injustice this side of paradise. It is better to stay and struggle than to hand over the store to those who have made a preferential option for prestige or the status quo."[15]

I am reminded that the things that are the most beautiful are often the most fragile and vulnerable, among them the original call and way we sought to live with one another in the neighborhood. The callings and

---

9. Cited in Myers, *Binding the Strong Man*.
10. Luke 11:24–26; see the discussion in Gill, *Life on the Road*, 208–10.
11. Myers, *Binding the Strong Man*.
12. Thurman, *Disciplines of the Spirit*, 1963.
13. Soelle, *Silent Cry*.
14. Williams, "On William Stringfellow."
15. Brackley, *Call to Discernment in Troubled Times*, 170.

charisms of a community require care and gentleness, a sense that they do not belong to us but to God, and therefore back to God they must always be returned. This is the paschal mystery, the birth, life, and death of Christ, and of Holy Saturday before the resurrection. It is in this story of the gospel message where we find our story in Sandtown, the source for imaginative renewal, of refounding.[16]

If community is that to which we aspire, sustaining the reality can be more difficult than the vision and the energy that created it. It is far easier to desire a "successful" church, school, or program, something we think we know how to assess, operate, or fix, but much riskier to find and continue in a new way to live and love. What matters most is presence and time, the trust and simplicity of life together.[17]

New Song did not "solve" the problems of systemic racism, urban abandonment, and structural injustice, but we lived in Christ where we were called to be. And by our witness to what is beautiful and good, we did bring about real changes, small differences that added up in big ways, and continue uniquely in the lives of each of us who had a part in this. As the Apostles' Creed invites us to live, we learned to heal what is broken, to look to God's life. Whether we had completed three houses or three hundred, this is what bearing witness to the kingdom looks like.

We are still New Song, a parable of the reign of God, a community of past and present, Black and white, young and old, unexpected friends, a picture in bits and pieces of the message of Jesus for everyone, broken and loving one another in a new communion. Wherever we are, each of us in this experience, whatever happens within us and among us, remains in fidelity to our calling of faith, hope, and love. By what took place in our lives, the trust, grace, and simplicity of our life together. Together we learned that we are no longer in bondage to death.

We had found purpose in our being together, communion with God, creation, and one another. We had given our lives to God's call, announcing a world beyond evictions, jails, divisions, and gun violence. Like the story of Ruth, we stayed with one another, embracing risks, each in our own way. As Orlando, who had been part of Sandtown Habitat from the early days shared, "It is a story I will be telling my grandchildren." Yes, a story of God

---

16. What this can mean for institutional life see the important work of Arbuckle, *Out of Chaos; Refounding the Church;* and *Catholic Identity.*

17. Scherz, *Having People, Having Heart.*

that needs to be remembered.[18] And a story of the energies of the Spirit that continues to move about in the city and world.

Empires of every size and type come and go, but there are a people in Sandtown who bear the fruit of the kingdom of God (Matthew 21:43). In words Allan loved, Nicholas Wolterstorff describes how our labors are the seeds of new creation, God's new world:

> Yet in the eschatological image of the city we have the assurance that our efforts to make these present cities of ours humane places in which to live—efforts which so often are frustrated, efforts which so often yield despair—will, by way of the mysterious patterns of history, eventually provide the tiles and timbers for a city of delight.[19]

The end of our journey is to God, where it began, with new creation. "Blessed are the meek, for they will inherit the earth" (Matthew 5:5), Jesus announced, a word for the neighborhood. Nothing done for the kingdom is lost.

For a sermon he delivered at New Song near the end of his life, Allan handwrote in the margins of his outline, "I have learned from being in Sandtown that to respond in love is like breathing, to not succumb to despair but 'Rise up!'" We are a resurrection people. Even now, seeds of peace are planted, watered by the Spirit who brings new life. Seeds that can grow in places we do not now see or expect. Seeds that will also grow and bloom for peace. Seeds born of Sandtown faith, ever resilient, prayerful, and watered in the love of God the Good Shepherd. Like grass through cement. The Lord is always inviting us to see a new reality, to be open to the good gift of grace.

Later in the stillness of this Christmas Day, I find myself standing alone next to 1385 North Gilmor Street, our first building, whose rebuilding was a sign of life for the neighborhood, but which is now once again a vacant husk. This is where Ike, Anton, Jermaine, and I, and countless others worked together to rebuild, where John Perkins spoke, where I preached and a church sang with joy, where the school started with Susan, Sonia, and Linda, where I met Rita as the health center operated in the basement, where Allan, LaVerne, and the guys ran Sandtown Habitat, and where Allan and I laughed and hung out on the ramp.

18. Davis, *Opening Israel's Scriptures*, 410.
19. Wolterstorff, *Until Justice and Peace Embrace*, 140.

Time

As I walk around Sandtown, I am filled with a spirit of gratitude, with thanksgiving to God.[20] Families are dwelling in their Sandtown Habitat homes; young people are finding a way forward at New Song Center. And if 1385 North Gilmor collapses or is torn down, the ruin will remain its own witness to this common life we shared, to the work we did together, and to the challenge of faith in our time and city. It will always be a place of vision and transformation.

I can now more clearly see the source of Allan being with me, as Sister Grace put it. When Love is grounded in communion with God, we know that even in death we are close to one another, and our hearts can be even more deeply united in the purpose and calling God created for us. "You have to trust," as the spiritual writer Henri Nouwen noted, "that every true friendship has no end, that a communion of saints exists among all those, living and dead, who have truly loved God and one another."[21]

As I consider the journey of writing this book, I recognize it as a reflection on St. Paul's hymn in the Letter to the Colossians, how "in him all things hold together."[22] Through the Creator, the cross, the urban church as the body of Christ, the world we see and don't see. Through God with us, a vision of the gospel of reconciliation and peace. And inasmuch as everything is connected and held together in Christ, however brief or long our lives are, beyond how we can comprehend space and time, there is an ever unfolding more within our stories and community in God. In the mystery of our dying and rising in Christ (Colossians 2:8–15). In the Love that just is.

Standing there at Gilmor and Laurens, I greet a family crossing the street to the Gilmor Homes. We do not know each other. "Are you going to fix up some of these houses?" they ask. We are now looking together at the bricks, timber, and plaster detritus from what had been a house next to the now abandoned church, and the one next to it hanging on by threads and strips of wood.

With their question, maybe a prayer from strangers, I realize it is now nearly full circle from the call that Allan and I shared to move to Sandtown as part of a gospel imperative; from a vision under a night sky; from a community drawing its dreams with crayons, then working and waiting for a

---

20. 1 Thessalonians 5:18

21. Nouwen, *Inner Voice of Love*, 81.

22. Colossians 1:15–20. For a larger and fuller perspective, see Williams, *Christ the Heart of Creation*. See also Imbelli, "Heart of the Matter."

miracle; watching a mountain of the Lord's house rise; a new song with the volume turned up.

It is Christmas, and we are each on our way to join our families. But there is a story to tell of the Word made flesh, God present in the neighborhood. About the Gospel of peace. So, I begin to tell, at least briefly, about a time of friendship and love, about a neighborhood of God called Sandtown.

Of a joy that has found a way. Amen.

Breath (Coda)

As I worked to complete this book, everything has seemed to reach its peak, and we find ourselves needing a different way. Does our story of a small Christian community in Sandtown offer a parable for these times? Does our experience in Sandtown provide a hopeful way of seeing, understanding, and engaging our world? What are the signs of the times that God invites to open our hearts to?

It began when the COVID-19 global pandemic struck. In New York City, during the first months, the sirens never seemed to stop, the losses for families and neighbors unspeakable, the most vulnerable indeed most vulnerable. Then it was everywhere around the world. A microbe was undoing public health systems, economies, and politics as we had known them. Breaking our social and emotional being.

COVID-19 is a universal cry for breath, but in the racial, geographic, and economic distribution of illness and health, inequalities and the failures of systems are exposed in death. For the virus especially preyed upon those who dwell in overcrowded housing, immigrant neighborhoods, upon the elderly, favelas, barrios, and informal settings of our urban world.[1] Places like Sandtown with broken or no health care systems, where the care received is not the care that is needed.

Breathe in. Breathe out. We are all watching our breath in a time of COVID.

Amidst this crisis, the planet is crying out, frying, trying to breathe. The planet, all of us, face an age of melting ice sheets, fierce heat, the orange cast of smoke from wildfires, water shortages, and once-every-hundred-year storms occurring every year. There is a crisis for marine life, the soil and food supply, for biodiversity. With our planet filled with toxic waste,

---

1. Making connections is Farmer, *Fevers, Feuds, and Diamonds*.

zones of exclusion, expanding places of abandonment, we are up against what the Scottish writer Cal Flyn calls the coming post-human landscape.[2]

The suffering of creation, cities and the world is a groaning, a crying out for the salvation and justice of God.[3] It is our home, and the home of God. I think of God breathing creation into being, of the same breath raising up bodies of the dead in the book of Ezekiel, of Jesus' loss of breath on the cross, of the breath of the living Spirit of God upon the church at Pentecost. Upon all of creation.[4]

And then we faced the presence of historic injustice. Breonna Taylor, a medical worker in Louisville, unarmed, a raid, a hail of police bullets, her breath taken away. And for eight minutes and forty-six seconds, centuries of injustice exposed once more. The knee of a Minneapolis police officer is pressed upon the neck of George Floyd until there is no more breath. The ever-present possibility of police violence if you are Black or Latino, every moment a matter of life and death.[5]

Demonstrations and prayers are then everywhere, with masks. Cyclists, too. City streets once empty now filled. Trying to breathe, the fire this time, James Baldwin being heard again. Saying the names, like Freddie Gray. And throughout, instruments playing, pots and pans banging at 7:00 PM each day for doctors, nurses, delivery workers. Signs of what can happen, if but for a moment. It is as if liturgy took to the streets.[6]

Our world is choking on weapons, as Bonhoeffer put it. We face new wars and a renewed global arms race and proliferation of nuclear weapons that may yet destroy our planet. And we know the slow-moving gun massacres in urban neighborhoods, an unspeakable violence and loss after loss, to now unspeakable gun massacres that seem to take place regularly in schools, places of worship, bowling alleys, and grocery stores. There is also ongoing anti-Asian American racism and violence across the nation.

We are in a polarizing time when people are being asked to take sides rather than listen, love thy neighbor, and live the gospel imperative. Nationalisms, many using religious language, are on the rise not just in America,

---

2. Flyn, *Islands of Abandonment*.

3. Jewett, *Romans*, 516–18. See also Keesmaat and Walsh, *Romans Disarmed*.

4. Copeland, "Breath and Fire," and Polter, "Reviving Our Common Life." See also Radcliffe, *Alive in God*, 262–79.

5. Boyd, "Police Violence and the Built Harm of Structural Racism."

6. On liturgy as action and as leading to the work of justice, see Wolterstorff, *Hearing the Call*.

Breath (Coda)

but globally.[7] With this are authoritarian leaders who are scapegoating difference and attacking the institutions of public life.

When we stop to consider all of this, we recognize that we are in a *kairos* moment, as Emmanuel Katongole points out, a specific time that asks us to go a different way, that invites us to see, discern, and act: Who are we to one another? How can we change? How can we collaborate? How can we achieve a better future for all humankind, God's dream for God's creation? Martin Luther King Jr.'s question about who we are to one another, rooted in justice and equality, remains essential: will we have chaos or community?

In this time, Pope Francis urges us forward with a bold yet easy-to-follow vision. We are to be a people of joy and hope for one another, for all of creation as our common home. Let us not give up on this hope; instead let us dream.[8] An integral ecology, connecting all things together, is the only way we can address our well-being, our health, our planet, Pope Francis writes in *Laudato Si'*. We must face that future now and with urgency, as he writes in *Laudato Deum*. Only together, in solidarity, in social friendship and trust, as Pope Francis also asks of us all, in *Fratelli Tutti*, do we have a future.

We also need communities and congregations of radical, biblical hope, of open friendship, as Jürgen Moltmann has urged. Love's presence, the Word made flesh, alive in neighborhoods, favelas, cities of every scale and size, especially in places of exclusion. Where the powers of death, in every sphere of life, are challenged in the power of the resurrection. Where Pentecost is the hope and horizon of a new church energized by the powers of God. The Spirit who breathes new life in a world that can't breathe.

We need the creation of new spaces and institutions for learning peace, community, accompaniment, mutuality, and discipleship. These point us, in the power of the Spirit, to hope, to the reign of God, and to Christ and creation, all of life connected. Spaces of nonviolence, beauty, and welcome. Settings for friendships to emerge and flourish. Where we can learn the gospel imperative, which is the kingdom of God.

Jeremiah 29:7–11 is addressed to people during a time of loss and uncertainty. But it invites us to something more radical than an action, mission, or strategy; it invites us to simply be neighbors, citizens of the city

---

7. Gorski and Perry, *Flag and the Cross*. For an account of how idolatry becomes possible, see Fowl, *Idolatry*.

8. Pope Francis, *Fratelli Tutti*; *Let us Dream*; and *Laudato Si'*.

and place where we are. It invites us to pray, raise our families, seek the well-being of our neighbors. It invites us to live in hope.⁹

It is a moment for a new generation of theologians to raise their voices and lead, from cities in Africa, Asia, Latin America, North America, and Europe, to speak into the twenty-first century. And for a new generation of artists, urbanists, economists, and shopkeepers to help us see and understand our times.

More than ever, we need young people to lift their voices. For the passion they bring to addressing matters of justice. For new ways of being church, and their journey of passing on faith to the next generation. To press new questions, to challenge, to make new things happen. To "stir things up," as Pope Francis said.

Because of COVID-19, global inequality, and the climate crisis, our bodies know that our well-being depends on the well-being of our neighbors, close and distant. We belong to a web of being, even as we find our world drawn into new divisions. For the good of all, we need a healthier and more just world. A commitment to sharing, not squandering, our years and resources. For seeing abundance not scarcity, for giving all we have to what matters. For an economic life that works for all. Only when we learn to put down our defenses and insecurities and to turn our swords into plowshares will we find human survival.¹⁰

In life, we often see "intractable" problems. Less often do we see, lift up, and work at alternatives, and do so with prayer and fasting. But change, as we found in Sandtown, only needs to begin with one person, two or three even, like an Ike, LaVerne, Nina, Jane, Mr. Kelley, Susan, or Allan, when we begin to realize that our whole center of gravity needs to shift.

When we recognize belonging together in friendship, and with all of creation. When our senses become alive to what is around us, to history and life. When we are converted to our neighbors, and we come to the place where we seek to live in a spirit of love, justice, and reconciliation.¹¹ When we realize something new is essential, we turn to steady, hard work of giving our all to what matters most deeply, entrusting all to God. Like in housing, neighborhood rebuilding, sustainability, walking alongside young people, as we sought in Sandtown. Here is a way of Christian witness and mission for our turbulent times.

---

9. For this setting, see O'Connor, *Jeremiah*.
10. Berrigan, *Isaiah*, 13.
11. Gutiérrez, *Theology of Liberation*, 205.

Breath (Coda)

If we face a time of loss, grief, and mourning in our cities and world, God's home, let us offer liturgies and lives of intercession, care, honor, remembrance, gratitude, confession, and anticipation for our common home, for our life together in God. For what can yet change. Mourning is something we carry with us, but its end is faith, hope, and love. And love, Dorothy Day reminds us, is the final witness.

If we live in a time of increasing "us versus them," "Us All," the words of Bruce Cockburn written during a time of COVID, is a song, a prayer that can help us to know who we are, the choices we must make. Will we build "shutters and walls" or find ourselves moving toward an "open embrace"? We each carry the scars of a broken world, but we still share a common humanity. All we have is "us all."[12]

Belonging together, loving one another, is our only possible future for flourishing life. We have a communion of saints from Sandtown to accompany us as we share our crust of bread with one another, to help us keep at it. We have the prophetic lives of King, Day, Perkins, and Romero to give us the language and vision to challenge the world as it is.[13] We have in the witness of saints across space and time the way of risk, sacrifice, and joy that is needed to build a different future for all God's people, creation, and creatures. They show us the way of humanness and holiness. They show us why we need the communion of saints.

Sandtown shows us, shows me, a way of God's hope in us, our common breath, a way of humanity and new creation. A way of rolling up our sleeves and doing the hard things. A way of sharing our crust of bread. A way of sharing our light all around our neighborhood!

I hear Sister Grace reminding me that Communion is all we have. Communion is all we need.

As Patti Smith sings in "People Have the Power,"

> Everything we dream
> can come to pass through our union.[14]

We can change things. The earth's revolution can be turned through belonging.

Sandtown, Elder Harris, leave us with both the question and invitation we need:

"Are you ready? Are you ready? Let's get to work!"

---

12. Bruce Cockburn, "Us All."
13. Williams, *Tokens*; Hagman, "Saints in Public."
14. Patti Smith and Fred "Sonic" Smith, "People Have the Power."

Afterword

Peter B. Price

"Man, I've just been arrested!" These were the first words I recall Mark Gornik speaking to me.

We were in El Salvador. It was 1988. Mark and I were part of a small delegation that had gone to offer solidarity to El Salvador's persecuted and suffering people and to learn about ecclesial life as they were living it during a war. On the first morning, Mark had been walking the streets of San Salvador, when armed government soldiers jumped out of a truck and surrounded him. After being questioned, he was released, unlike so many other people at the time.

This was the first time we met. For the next few days we walked city favelas, travelled through the countryside visiting with people who had been displaced by the war, and met with base ecclesial communities. Mark and I became friends. I also had the opportunity to listen to him tell the beginnings of the story which he has recorded in this remarkable book.

Sharing the Crust is a testimony of inspired individuals who together built Christian community as a place where people grow in love and peacemaking, in an area of West Baltimore that could, sadly, be compared to the violence and despair we had witnessed in El Salvador. It was some six months after returning from Central America that I visited Sandtown and met Allan Tibbels. He was everything and more that Mark had described in the back of the truck as we drove through in the El Salvador hills. What I witnessed in Sandtown was a vision of simple, radical Christian faith by which people were seeking to live.

During my first visit, Mark took me to the roof of their future church and community center, at 1385 North Gilmor Street, that he writes about

Afterword

in this book. The long-abandoned building was nowhere near renovated, but Mark didn't see it that way. "Look, we have a new roof," he said with excitement. "In six months, we are going to finish and dedicate this building." Little chance, I thought. But how wrong I was. The deadline was met and a vision of a renewed neighborhood with rehabbed houses revealed a commitment to hope and faith. House by house, block by block things changed. Hope was kindled. Faith rewarded.

Sharing the Crust not only tells the story of a very special relationship between individuals committed to a vision of building community, but of deep friendship as the secret of serving Christ in the city. Mark describes this friendship as "a sacrament of vulnerability."

The accident that rendered Allan a quadriplegic and led to almost total paralysis is an event that would have given most people a "pass" in God's sight to undertake the lightest of service. As Mark's story unfolds, we are instead faced with the picture of Allan as a man of the most extraordinary faith, fortitude, and courage. Together with Susan, without whom Allan could not have taken the journey that this book recounts, they left comparative comfort and well-being for the uncertainty of a new urban environment.

The style of leadership that Mark describes is one in which everyone is valued. Their opinions, contribution, vision, and insights are all seen to be important in discerning the way forward. Offering such leadership is very difficult and comes from God as a gift. Church leaders, like their secular counterparts, can all too easily allow their egos and self-importance to cloud the vision, and to cut out the other voices of those whom God has given gifts for the work of ministry.

Jesus defined his leadership as that of a servant: "I am among you as one who serves" (Luke 22:27) he says. Immediately following this, Jesus reflected to his hearers, "You are the ones who have stood by me in my trials; and I confer on you, just as my Father has conferred on me, a kingdom."

The story of Sandtown that you have just read is the story of such people. The kingdom vision that caught the fire of imagination and became the "community of friends" included those both within and without the church community, yet somehow everything became truly ecclesial. They sought to live an understanding of the kingdom of God where everything is connected for the well-being of creation and resist all that undermines God's image revealed in humanity.

Afterword

Sharing the Crust is a story for our times. Profoundly inspiring, it is one of the most incredible beauty, challenge, and hope.

The Rt Revd Peter B. Price
London, England

> *Peter B. Price, an author and broadcaster, was formerly Bishop of Bath and Wells. A founder of New Ways of Being Church in England, he is the author of numerous books, including* Things That Make for Peace: A Christian Peacemaker in a World of War *(Darton, Longman and Todd) and* A Shaking Reality: Daily Reflections for Advent *(Darton, Longman and Todd/Fortress). Peter lives in London with his wife, Dee. He is known for his global work for reconciliation in places of conflict and violence.*

Acknowledgments

It took a communion of saints to tell this story. The gratitude of my heart to Sandtown, Baltimore, and everyone who rolled up your sleeves, lent a hand, prayed, learned how to use a hammer the right way, planted gardens, cheered, sang along, shared your loaves and fishes, walked with students, filled a dumpster, and built a life together.

Susan, who trusted me with Allan's story, and kept telling me to get it done.

Ike, for his witness and friendship from the first.

Allen, Jenny, Jessica, Brandon, Gary, and Fitt, of course!

Rita, Peter, and Daniel for the crazy life and laughter we share, for the journey we are on, the sports we debate (I'm usually right, of course), for the faith we are learning to know and live.

My mother, Sally Gornik, and my late father, Ray, for loving me, praying for me, and sending me to youth group. And to Susan and Karen, Thomas and Bo. To Ildiko, Attila, and our Hungarian family near and far, including Zoli and Kata, Reka and Zsolt, Peter and Kinga. We remember Adorjan, Janos, Ilona.

Bishop Peter Price, for talking over and working through the entirety of this story with me. For his kindness in writing the afterword. For the generosity of his friendship. For all I am still learning from him.

Sister Grace Myerjack, for her role in my formation and story, for walking with me and sharing the experience of Christ, and the Maryknoll Sisters, for their witness and prayers.

John Perkins, for writing the foreword, for taking the risk of Voice of Calvary, and for his care for Sandtown and me. Thank you too, Priscilla Perkins.

Acknowledgments

Andrew and Ingrid Walls, for friendship, and cheering and shaping this along the way, for discussions about the saints and powers. Thank you, Andrew, for sending me Aberdeen Iggy.

Willa Bickham for generosity of spirit and amazing creation that graces the cover, and to Willa, Brendan Walsh, and Viva House on South Mount Street for your witness. It is good to know we were neighbors, and still are at a distance.

Bethia Liu for always showing a way to tell the story.

Charles Marsh, Karen Marsh, and the Project on Lived Theology at the University of Virginia for an exciting and welcoming context of support and encouragement over the years. I am especially grateful to the Virginia Seminar group of Charles Marsh, Carlos Eire, Patricia Hampl, Susan Holman, Alan Jacobs, and Charles Mathewes.

Steve Fowl, for friendship and wisdom that continues to be a gift.

Chris Coble, Brian Williams, and everyone at Lilly Endowment for your deep care for pastors, ministry, and congregational life in cities. And for the blessed memory of John Wimmer.

City Seminary companions Miriam and Peter Acevedo, Marjie and Bruce Calvert, Sue Baker, Maria and Tony Wong, Bola Oyesanya, Adrienne Croskey and family, Adebisi and Abby Oyesile, Vivian and Beverly Grubb, Geomon and Reji George, Sister Marylin Gramas, Huibing He, Sue Baker, Robert McInnis, Sarah Gerth van den Berg, Afia Sun Kim, Rex Agyemang, Hannah Newman-Pan, Christy Choi, Derrick Miu, Tony Shaw, Susan Post, Kari Jo Cates, and Biju George.

Robert Embry, for walking with us and his heart for Baltimore.

Skip Masback, friend, pastor, advocate, and teacher, holder of Sandtown memories. And thank you, Amy.

Roger Young for remembering our long story.

Eugene, Grace, Weston, Nate, Carolina, and Scout!

Miroslav Volf for his years of encouragement and invitation to join in projects at the Yale Center for Faith and Culture.

St. Connell, nice hoverboard and Lou Reed music.

Hannah Newman-Pan who gave this many expert readings and encouragement along the way, then took up many a task to getting this out the door. Three cheers! And again, more cheers. Thank you, Hazel, too! I am grateful.

Emmanuel Katongole, Sister Marylin, and Steve Fowl too for their many insights into early versions of this story. Sarah Gerth van den Berg for an early reading and important feedback. Ulrike Guthrie who helped

Acknowledgments

me see this story across a finish line, at just the right time and with kindness and generosity of spirit.

Mike Barb, LaVerne Stokes, Al Stokes, Renay Kelley, Sister Marylin, Steve Fowl, and Isaac Newman, Jessica Moss, for all you shared. The great Roland Freeman for insights and images.

Bob Wells, and Duke Faith and Leadership, for an early opportunity to write about Allan and Sandtown. Brian Walsh, for first inviting me to talk about this story in Toronto, Canada, a most memorable time.

The Cathedral of the Incarnation, The Freeloaders Club, The Carmelite Sisters of Baltimore, Loyola University Maryland, New Shiloh Baptist Church, Fresh Oils Ministries, St. Edward the Martyr, Nick Wolterstorff, Anita, Linda, the late Senator Paul Sarbanes for his generous spirit and commitment to Sandtown, the Sarbanes family for their care and public spirit in Baltimore, Dan and Kay Broadwater, Arnie Graf, Antero Pietila, Jim Bock, Sam Tran, Carmen Ortiz, Jeff and Rebecca, Mary Ann Bell, Ellen Janes, Parris Glendening, Tom Gamper, Dr. Wesner, Rev. Al Stokes, Gary Tibbels, Dr. Denisch, Bill Frey, Jim and Patty Rouse, Pat Costigan, Mother Cooper, Bart Harvey, Spirit and Truth, Blanca Ortiz, Rudy and Collyn Schmidt, James Ward, Covenant College, Steve Lutz, Reginald McLelland, the taxi drivers of Dakar and Edinburgh, Bob Boluter, Chris Scharen, The Gates, Guillermo Cook, Jack, Winston and Maureen, Charlie Horn, Bob Aronson, Jim Wallis, the announcers for the New York Yankees John and Suzyn, Stanley Hauerwas for thoughts on friendship, John Kiess, Walt Frazier, Tremper Longman, the art of Jacob Lawrence, Rimmer deVries, Ray Bakke, Elizabeth Conde-Frazier, Jon Pott, Kurt L. Schmoke, Lisa Greenhouse of Enoch Pratt Free Library, Clergy United for the Transformation of Sandtown (CUTS), Doreen Kellogg, Roger Haight, SJ, Slovenia, Canada, Ken Haron, John and Clare Armes, Inigo, Pierre, Francis, Jorge, and Swanson TV dinners.

David Bratt and Laura Bardolph for saying no when this book wasn't ready, and then for cultivating the more that it became. Michael Thomson for taking on this book. Wonderful to be working together again! Thank you Rodney Clapp, Shannon Carter, Heather Carraher, and everyone at Wipf and Stock.

Bruce Cockburn for his unique grace in our story, U2, and Patti Smith for music of the Spirit and life.

Shadow, a gentle companion to our family who watched over the first pages of this book. To the peaceable kingdom we give you, and Tungba.

Acknowledgments

Ignacio continues the story, present for the last pages, bringing much laughter, along with the occasional crime scene and jelly donut. And yes of course, I am also Franciscan.

Allan, I hope you like this, especially the playlist and commas. Allan, Mamie, LaVerne, please pray for me, for us. For the Knicks, too. And to all, life is short, so call now.

As Willa Bickham explains the cover image painted with Julia Walsh-Little, the shafts of wheat and the bread in the front of the row houses are symbols of sharing and communion; the brightness in front is to shine light on the work of New Song; the hand is for the humanity of the story lived; and the flowers convey the love that was expressed.

Willa and her husband Brendan Walsh founded Viva House, a part of the Catholic Worker Movement, on South Mount Street in Baltimore, where for over fifty years they have continued to live in hospitality.

Further Resources / Bibliography

Listen (playlist)

This playlist represents music that accompanies the text and the journey we experienced, part of the times we lived. The playlist is available on Spotify under *Sharing the Crust*.

Sonny Rollins, Sonny Stitt, and Dizzy Gillespie. "On the Sunny Side of the Street." *Sonny Side Up*. Verve Music, 1986.
Bruce Cockburn. "Santiago Dawn." *World of Wonders*. True North Records, 1986.
Marian Anderson. "My Lord, What a Morning." *Marian Anderson Sings Great Spirituals*. Sony Music, 1948, 2021.
Bruce Cockburn. "Joy will Find a Way." *Joy Will Find a Way*. True North Records, 1975.
Taizé. "Jesus Christ, Bread of Life." *Mane Nobiscum*. Ateliers et Presses de Taizé, 2010.
Bruce Cockburn, "To Fit in My Heart." *Life Short Call Now*. True North Records, 2006.
John Coltrane. *A Love Supreme*. Verve Music, 1965.
Bruce Cockburn. "Shipwrecked at the Stable Door." *Big Circumstance*. True North Records, 1989.
U2. "Magnificent." *No Line on the Horizon*. Island Records, 2009.
Bruce Cockburn. "Lord of the Starfields." *In the Falling Dark*. High Romance Music, 1976.
Midnight Oil. "Beds are Burning." *Diesel and Dust*. Midnight Oil Ents Pty Ltd, 1987.
Hezekiah Walker. "I Need You." *The Essential Hezekiah Walker*. Zomba Recording, 2002.
Taizé. "The Kingdom of God." *Laudate Omnes Gentes*. GIA, 2002.
Public Enemy. "Fight the Power." *Fear of a Black Planet*. Def Jam Records, 1990.
Bruce Cockburn. "If a Tree Falls in the Forest." *Big Circumstance*. High Romance Music, 1989.
U2. "40." *War*. Island Records, 1983.
Curtis Mayfield. "People Get Ready." *Curtis/Live!*. Warner Strategic Marketing, 1971.
Charlie Haden and Hank Jones. "Precious Lord, Take My Hand." *Steal Away*. Decca Records France, 1995.
Bruce Cockburn. "Waiting for a Miracle." *Waiting for a Miracle*. True North Records, 1987.
Yousou N'Dour, "Immigrés." *I Bring What I Love*. Nonesuch Records, 2010.
Kendrick Lamar "Feel." *Damn*. Aftermath Entertainment/ Interscope Records, 2017.
Beethoven. "String Quartet in C Sharp Minor."

Further Resources / Bibliography

Bruce Cockburn. "Isn't That What Friends Are For?" *Breakfast in New Orleans, Dinner in Timbuktu*. True North Records, 1999.
Dan Schutte. "Pilgrim Companions." *Drawn by a Dream*. OCP, 1993.
Aretha Franklin. "What a Friend We Have in Jesus." *Amazing Grace: The Complete Recordings Live*. Atlantic Recording, 1972.
Bruce Cockburn. "Festival of Friends." *In the Falling Dark*. True North Records, 1976.
Patti Smith. "Paths that Cross." *Dream of Life*. Arista Records, 1992.
Bruce Cockburn. "Cry of a Tiny Babe." *Nothing But a Burning Light*. True North Records, 1991.
U2. "One Step Closer." *How to Dismantle an Atomic Bomb*. Island Records, 2004.
Bruce Cockburn. "Open." *You've Never Seen Everything*. True North Records, 2003.
Taizé "Veni, Sancte Spiritus." *Music of Unity and Peace*. Deutsche Grammaphon GmbH, 2015.
U2. "Pride (In the Name of Love)." *The Unforgettable Fire*. Island Records, 1984.
Bruce Cockburn. "Us All." *O Sun O Moon*. True North Records, 2023.
Patti Smith and Fred "Sonic" Smith. "People Have the Power." *Dream of Life*. Arista Records, 1988.
The Montgomery Improvement Association. "This Little Light of Mine." *Sing for Freedom*. Smithsonian Folkways Recordings, 1990.

See

David Simon. *The Wire*. HBO, 2002–2008.
Marylin Ness. *Charm City*. PBS, 2019.
David Simon and George Pelecanos. *We Own This City*. HBO, 2022.

Read

Adichie, Chimamanda Ngozi. *Notes on Grief*. New York: Knopf, 2021.
Aguirre, Jessica Camille. "How to Recycle a 14-story Office Tower." *New York Times*, October 6, 2022. https://www.nytimes.com/2022/10/06/headway/office-tower-carbon-emissions-amsterdam.html.
al-Sabouni, Marwa. *Building for Hope: Towards an Architecture of Belonging*. London: Thames & Hudson, 2021.
Arbuckle, Gerald A. *Catholic Identity or Identities? Refounding Ministries in Chaotic Times*. Collegeville, MN: Liturgical, 2013.
———. *Earthing the Gospel: An Inculturation Handbook for the Pastoral Worker*. Maryknoll, NY: Orbis, 1990.
———. *Out of Chaos: Refounding Religious Communities*. London: Geoffrey Chapman, 1988.
———. *Refounding the Church: Dissent for Leadership*. Maryknoll, NY: Orbis, 1993.
Arias, Mortimer. *Announcing the Reign of God: Evangelization and the Subversive Memory of Jesus*. Philadelphia: Fortress, 1984.
Arrupe, Pedro. *Essential Writings*. Selected by Kevin Burke. Maryknoll, NY: Orbis, 2004.
Augustine. *The Confessions of St. Augustine*. Translated by F. J. Sheed. New York: Sheed and Ward, 1943.
Banerjee, Abhijit V., and Esther Duflo. *Poor Economics: A Radical Rethinking of the Way to Fight Global Poverty*. New York: Public Affairs, 2011.

Further Resources / Bibliography

Barclay, John M. G. *Paul and the Gift*. Grand Rapids: Eerdmans, 2015.
Barnes, Michael. *Waiting on Grace: A Theology of Dialogue*. Oxford: Oxford University Press, 2020.
Barth, Markus. *The Broken Wall: A Study of the Epistle to the Ephesians*. Valley Forge, PA: Judson, 1959.
Bennett, Lerone, Jr. *Before the Mayflower*. Chicago: Johnson, 1962.
Berrigan, Daniel, SJ. *Isaiah: Spirit of Courage, Gifts of Tears*. Minneapolis: Fortress, 1996.
———. *Jeremiah: The World, The Wound of God*. Minneapolis: Fortress, 1999.
———. *Love, Love at the End: Parables, Prayers and Meditations*. New York: MacMillan, 1968.
———. *The Mission: A Film Journal*. San Francisco: Harper and Row, 1986.
———. *To Dwell in Peace: An Autobiography*. San Francisco: Harper and Row, 1987.
Berrigan, Philip, and Elizabeth McAlister. *The Time's Discipline: The Beatitudes and Nuclear Resistance*. Baltimore: Fortkamp, 1989.
Berrigan, Philip. *A Ministry of Risk: Writings on Peace and Nonviolence*. Edited by Brad Wolf. New York: Fordham University Press, 2024.
Bethge, Eberhard. *Friendship and Resistance: Essays on Dietrich Bonhoeffer*. Geneva: WCC/Grand Rapids: Eerdmans, 1995.
Bevans, Stephen. *Community of Missionary Disciples: The Continuing Creation of the Church*. Maryknoll, NY: Orbis, forthcoming.
———. "Pope Francis's Missiology of Attraction," *International Bulletin of Missionary Research* 43:1 (2019) 20–28.
Blaine, Keisha N. *Until I am Free: Fannie Lou Hammer's Enduring Message to America*. Boston: Beacon, 2021.
Bock, James. "People Find a Voice with New Song." *The Evening Sun*, December 17, 1994.
Boff, Leonard. *Ecclesiogenesis: The Base Communities Reinvent the Church*. Maryknoll, NY: Orbis, 1986.
Bondi, Roberta. *To Pray and to Love: Conversations on Prayer with the Early Church*. Minneapolis: Fortress, 1991.
Bonhoeffer, Dietrich. *Ethics*. Translated by Reinhard Krauss, Charles C. West, and Douglass W. Stott. Dietrich Bonhoeffer Works 6. Minneapolis: Fortress, 2005.
———. *Letters and Papers from Prison*. Dietrich Bonhoeffer Works 8. Translated by Isabel Best, Lisa E. Dahill, Reinhard Krauss, and Nancy Lukens. Minneapolis: Fortress, 2009.
———. *Life Together and Prayerbook of the Bible*. Dietrich Bonhoeffer Works 5. Translated by Daniel W. Bloesch and James H. Burtness. Minneapolis: Fortress, 2004.
———. *Sanctorum Communio: A Theological Study of the Sociology of the Church*. Dietrich Bonhoeffer Works, vol. 1. Translated by Reinhard Krauss and Nancy Lukens. Minneapolis: Fortress, 1998.
Bouma-Prediger, Steven, and Brian J. Walsh. *Beyond Homelessness: Christian Faith in a Culture of Displacement*. Updated ed. Grand Rapids: Eerdmans, 2023.
Bouwsma, William J. *John Calvin: A Sixteenth-Century Portrait*. New York: Oxford University Press, 1988.
Boyd, Rhea W. "Police Violence and the Built Harm of Structural Racism." *The Lancet*, vol. 392, July 28, 2018, 258–59.
Boyle, Gregory. *Barking to the Choir: The Power of Radical Kinship*. New York: Simon and Schuster, 2017.

Further Resources / Bibliography

Brackley, Dean, SJ. *The Call to Discernment in Troubled Times: New Perspectives on the Transformative Wisdom of Ignatius of Loyola*. New York: Crossroad, 2004.

———. "Downward Mobility: Social Implications of St. Ignatius's Two Standards." *Studies in the Spirituality of the Jesuits* 20:1 (January 1988) 1–50.

Branch, Taylor. *Parting the Waters: America in the King Years 1954–63*. New York: Simon and Schuster, 1988.

Bretherton, Luke. *Christ and the Common Life: Political Theology and the Case for Democracy*. Grand Rapids: Eerdmans, 2019.

Brett, Mark G. *Political Trauma and Healing: Biblical Ethics for a Postcolonial World*. Grand Rapids: Eerdmans, 2016.

Brinig, Margaret F., and Nicole Stelle Garnett. *Lost Classroom, Lost Community: Catholic Schools' Importance in Urban America*. Chicago: University of Chicago Press, 2015.

Broadwater, Luke, and Ian Duncan. "Neighborhoods are Crying Out." *Baltimore Sun*, September 25, 2018.

Broom, Sarah M. *The Yellow House*. New York: Grove, 2019.

Brown, Lawrence T. *The Black Butterfly: The Harmful Politics of Race and Space in America*. Baltimore: Johns Hopkins University Press, 2021.

Brown, Peter. *The Cult of the Saints: Its Rise and Function in Latin Christianity*. Enlarged ed. Chicago: University of Chicago Press, 2015.

———. *Poverty and Leadership in the Later Roman Empire*. Hanover, NH: Brandeis University Press/Historical Society of Israel, 2002.

Butler, Anthea. *White Evangelical Racism: The Politics of Morality in America*. Chapel Hill: University of North Carolina Press, 2021.

Calvert, Scott, "Brick by Brick, Baltimore's Blighted Houses Get a New Life." *The Wall Street Journal*, April 5, 2019. https://www.wsj.com/articles/brick-by-brick-baltimores-blighted-houses-get-a-new-life-11554472800.

Carter, J. Kameron. *Race: A Theological Account*. New York: Oxford University Press, 2008.

CHARM: Voices of Baltimore Youth. *Homegrown: A Message to Baltimore by Baltimore*. Baltimore: CHARM, 2022.

Chittister, Joan. *Radical Spirit: 12 Ways to Live a Free and Authentic Life*. New York: Convergent, 2017.

Coates, Ta-Nehisi. *The Beautiful Struggle*. New York: Spiegel and Grau, 2008.

———. *Between the World and Me*. New York: Spiegel and Grau, 2015.

———. "The Black Family in the Age of Mass Incarceration." *The Atlantic*, October 2015, 60–84.

Cole, Teju. *Known and Strange Things*. New York: Random House, 2016.

Coles, Robert. *Dorothy Day: A Radical Devotion*. Redding, MA: Addison-Wesley, 1987.

Conde-Frazier, Elizabeth. "From Hospitality to Shalom." In *A Many Colored Kingdom: Multicultural Dynamics for Spiritual Formation*, edited by Elizabeth Conde-Frazier, S. Steve Kang, and Gary A. Parrett ,167–210. Grand Rapids: Baker Academic, 2004.

Cone, James H. *The Cross and the Lynching Tree*. Maryknoll, NY: Orbis, 2011.

———. *God of the Oppressed*. New York: Seabury, 1975.

———. *Martin and Malcom and America: A Dream of a Nightmare*. Maryknoll, NY: Orbis, 1991.

———. *Said I Wasn't Gonna Tell Nobody*. Maryknoll, NY: Orbis, 2018.

Cook, Guillermo. *The Expectation of the Poor: Latin American Basic Ecclesial Communities in Protestant Perspective*. Maryknoll, NY: Orbis, 1985.

Further Resources / Bibliography

———. "The Protestant Predicament: From Base Ecclesial Community to Established Church—A Brazilian Case Study. *International Bulletin of Missionary Research*, July 1984, 98–104.
Copeland, Shawn M. "Breath and Fire." *Commonweal*, July 2020. https://www.commonwealmagazine.org/breath-fire.
Costas, Orlando E. *Christ Outside the Gate: Mission Beyond Christendom.* Maryknoll: Orbis, 1982.
Croasmun, Matthew, and Miroslav Volf. *The Hunger for Home: Food and Meals in the Gospel of Luke.* Waco, TX: Baylor University Press, 2022.
Crosby, Michael H. *House of Disciples: Church, Economics, and Justice in Matthew.* Maryknoll, NY: Orbis, 1988.
Curtis, Jesse. *The Myth of Colorblind Christians: Evangelicals and White Supremacy in the Civil Rights Era.* New York: NYU Press, 2021.
Danticat, Edwidge. *The Art of Death: Writing the Final Story.* Minneapolis: Graywolf, 2017.
———. *Brother, I'm Dying.* New York: Alfred A. Knopf, 2007.
Davis, Ellen F. *Opening Israel's Scriptures.* New York: Oxford University Press, 2019.
———. *Biblical Prophecy: Perspectives for Christian Theology, Discipleship, and Ministry.* Louisville: Westminster John Knox, 2014.
Day, Dorothy. *The Long Loneliness.* New York: Harper & Row, 1981.
———. *Thérèse.* Notre Dame: Christian Classics, 2016.
Daymond, Antonia Michelle, Frederick L. Ware, and Eric Lewis Williams, eds. *T&T Clark Handbook of African American Theology.* London: T&T Clark, 2019.
Dayton, Donald W. *Discovering an Evangelical Heritage.* New York: Harper & Row, 1976.
Dear, John. *The Gospel of Peace: A Commentary on Matthew, Mark, and Luke from the Perspective of Nonviolence.* Maryknoll: Orbis, 2024.
DeGruchy, John W. *Cry Justice: Prayers, Meditations and Readings from South Africa.* Maryknoll, NY: Orbis, 1986
———. *Led into Mystery: Faith Seeking Answers in Life and Death.* London: SCM, 2013.
DeLuca, Stefanie, et al. *Coming of Age in the Other America.* New York: Russell Sage Foundation, 2016.
DeParle, Jason. "Wheelchair Missionary." *The New York Times Magazine*, December 26, 2010, 30–31.
DeSalvo, Louise. *Writing as a Way of Healing: How Telling Our Stories Transforms our Lives.* Boston: Beacon, 1999.
Desmond, Matthew. *Evicted: Poverty and Profit in the American City.* New York: Crown, 2016.
———. *Poverty, By America.* New York: Crown, 2023.
Didion, Joan. *Year of Magical Thinking.* New York: Knopf, 2005.
Dochuk, Darren, et al. *American Evangelicalism: George Marsden and the State of American Religious History.* Notre Dame: University of Notre Dame Press, 2014.
Douglas, Kelley Brown. *Resurrection Hope: A Future Where Black Lives Matter.* Maryknoll, NY: Orbis, 2021.
Dubler, Joshua, and Vincent Lloyd. *Break Every Yoke: Religion, Justice and the Abolition of Prisons.* New York: Oxford University Press, 2020.
Eareckson, Joni. *Joni.* New York: Bantam, 1976.
Edwards, Elise M. "A Womanist Consideration of Architecture and the Common Good." *Journal of the Society of Christian Ethics* 40:2 (Fall/Winter 2020) 252–72.

Further Resources / Bibliography

Eire, Carlos. *Reformations: The Early Modern World, 1450–1650*. New Haven: Yale University Press, 2016.

———. *A Very Brief History of Eternity*. Princeton: Princeton University Press, 2010.

Ellsberg, Robert. *All Saints: Daily Reflections on Saints, Prophets and Witnesses for our Time*. New York: Crossroad, 1997.

———. *Blessed Among Us: Day by Day with Saintly Witnesses*. Collegeville, MN: Liturgical Press, 2016.

———. *A Living Gospel: Reading God's Story in Holy Lives*. Maryknoll, NY: Orbis, 2019.

Ellul, Jacques. *Violence: Reflections from a Christian Perspective*. New York: Seabury, 1969.

Engelke, Matthew. *How to Think Like an Anthropologist*. Princeton: Princeton University Press, 2018.

Ercolano, Patrick. "Interracial Ministry is Fused with Love." *The Evening Sun*, August 15, 1989.

Farmer, Paul. *Fevers, Feuds, and Diamonds: Ebola and the Ravages of History*. New York: Farrar, Straus and Giroux, 2020.

———. *Pathologies of Power: Health, Human Rights, and the New War on the Poor*. Berkeley: University of California Press, 2003.

Farmer, Paul, and Gustavo Gutiérrez. *In the Company of the Poor: Conversations with Dr. Paul Farmer and Fr. Gustavo Gutiérrez*. Edited by Michael Griffin and Jennie Weiss Block. Maryknoll, NY: Orbis, 2013.

Fergusson, David. *The Providence of God: A Polyphonic Approach*. Cambridge: Cambridge University Press, 2018.

Finnerty, Adam. *No More Plastic Jesus: Global Justice and Christian Lifestyle*. Maryknoll, NY: Orbis, 1977.

Florer-Bixler, Melissa. *Fire by Night: Finding God in the Pages of the Old Testament*. Harrisonburg, PA: Herald, 2019.

Flyn, Cal. *Islands of Abandonment: Nature Rebounding in the Post-Human Landscape*. New York: Viking, 2021.

Ford, David F. *Christian Wisdom: Desiring God and Learning in Love*. Cambridge: Cambridge University Press, 2007.

———. *The Gospel of John: A Theological Commentary*. Grand Rapids: Baker, 2021.

———. *Self and Salvation: Being Transformed*. Cambridge: Cambridge University Press, 1999.

Forest, Jim. *At Play in the Lion's Den: A Biography and Memoir of Daniel Berrigan*. Maryknoll, NY: Orbis, 2017.

Fowl, Stephen E. *Ephesians: A Commentary*. Louisville: Westminster John Knox, 2012.

———. *Idolatry*. Waco, TX: Baylor University Press, 2019.

———. *Philippians*. Grand Rapids: Eerdmans, 2005.

Fowler, Robert Booth. *A New Engagement: Evangelical Political Thought, 1966–1976*. Grand Rapids: Eerdmans, 1982.

Francis, Pope. *Evangelii Gaudium*. 2013.

———. *Fratelli tutti*. 2020.

———. *Laudato Deum*. 2023.

———. *Laudato Si'*. 2015.

———. *Let us Dream: The Path to a Better Future*. New York: Simon and Schuster, 2020.

———. *Maiorem Hac Dilectionem (On the Offer of Life)*. 2017.

Freeman, Roland L. *The Arabbers of Baltimore*. Centreville, MD: Tidewater, 1989.

Freire, Paul. *Pedagogy of the Oppressed*. New York: Herder and Herder, 1972.

Further Resources / Bibliography

Gill, Athol. *Life on the Road: The Gospel Basis for a Messianic Lifestyle.* Homebush West, NSW: Lancer, 1989.

Girard, René. *When These Things Begin: Conversations with Michel Treguer.* East Lansing, MI: Michigan State University Press, 2014.

Glaude, Eddie S., Jr. *Begin Again: James Baldwin's America and Its Urgent Lessons for our Own.* New York: Crown, 2020.

González, Justo. *For the Healing of the Nations: The Book of Revelation in an Age of Cultural Conflict.* Maryknoll, NY: Orbis, 2005.

Gornik, Mark R. *To Live in Peace: Biblical Faith and the Changing Inner City.* Grand Rapids: Eerdmans, 2002.

———. *Word Made Global: Stories of African Christianity in New York City.* Grand Rapids: Eerdmans, 2005.

Gornik, Mark R., and Maria Liu Wong. *Stay in the City: How Christian Faith is Flourishing in an Urban World.* Grand Rapids: Eerdmans, 2017.

Gorski, Philip S., and Samuel L. Perry. *The Flag and the Cross: White Christian Nationalism and the Threat to American Democracy.* New York: Oxford University Press, 2022.

Gratz, Roberta Brandes. *The Living City.* New York: Simon and Schuster, 1989.

Green, Erica L. "Hundreds Bid Farewell to Sandtown Leader." *The Baltimore Sun*, June 15, 2010.

Griffith, Aaron. *God's Law and Order: The Politics of Punishment in Evangelical America.* Cambridge: Harvard University Press, 2020.

Gunderson, Gary, et al. "Faith-Based Assets and Multi-Sector Community Teams: Tapping into Deeply Woven Roots." *North Carolina Medical Journal* 79:4 (July–August 2018) 236–37.

Gutiérrez, Gustavo. *On Job: God-Talk and the Suffering of the Innocent.* Maryknoll, NY: Orbis, 1987.

———. *Spiritual Writings: Selected with an Introduction by Daniel G. Groody.* Maryknoll, NY: Orbis, 2011.

———. *A Theology of Liberation: History, Politics, and Salvation.* Maryknoll, NY: Orbis, 1973.

Hager, Eli. "There Are Still 80 'Youth Prisons' in the U.S. Here Are Five Things You Need to Know About Them." *The Marshall Project.* https://www.themarshallproject.org/2016/03/03/there-are-still-80-youth-prisons-in-the-u-s-here-are-five-things-to-know-about-them.

Hagman, Patrik. "Saints in Public: Holy Lives and the Function of Theological Speech in the Political Theology of Rowan Williams." *Studia Theologica—Nordic Journal of Theology*, 2021, 1–24.

Hamley, Isabell. *Embracing Justice.* London: SPCK, 2021.

Harding, Vincent. *There is a River: The Black Struggle for Freedom in America.* New York: Vintage, 1983.

Hatch, John W., with the help of Anne E. Callan, Eugenia Eng, and Curtis Jackson. "The General Baptist State Convention Health and Human Services Project." *Contact* 77 (February 1984).

Hauerwas, Stanley. "Friendship and Freedom: Reflections on Bonhoeffer's 'The Friend,'" In *Working with Words: On Learning to Speak Christian*, 270–85. Eugene, OR: Cascade, 2011.

Hayhoe, Katharine. *Saving Us: A Climate Scientist's Hope and Healing for a Divided World.* New York: One Signal/Atria, 2021.

Further Resources / Bibliography

Hennessy, Kate. *Dorothy Day: The World Will Be Saved by Beauty, An Intimate Portrait of My Grandmother*. New York: Scribner, 2017.

Heschel, Abraham J. *The Prophets*. Philadelphia: Jewish Publication Society, 1962.

Hinton, Elizabeth. *America on Fire: The Untold History of Police Violence and Black Rebellion Since the 1960s*. New York: Liveright, 2021.

———. *From the War on Poverty to the War on Crime: The Making of Mass Incarceration in America*. Cambridge: Harvard University Press, 2016.

Holman, Susan R. *God Knows There's Need: Christian Responses to Poverty*. New York: Oxford University Press, 2009.

Holton, M. Jan. *Longing for Home: Forced Displacement and the Postures of Hospitality*. New Haven: Yale University Press, 2016.

Hong, Cathy Park. *Minor Feelings: An Asian American Reckoning*. New York: One World, 2020.

Hood, Walter, and Grace Mitchell Tada. *Black Landscapes Matter*. Charlottesville: University of Virginia Press, 2020.

Hoornaert, Eduardo. *The Memory of the Christian People*. Maryknoll, NY: Orbis, 1988.

Hope, Anne, and Sally Timmel. *Training for Transformation: A Handbook for Community Workers*, books 1–3. Gweru, Zimbabwe: Mambo, 1984.

Hope, Anne, and Sally Timmel, eds. *Training for Transformation in Practice*. Warwickshire, UK: Practical Action Publishing, 2014.

Imbelli, Robert. "The Heart of the Matter." *America*, April 1, 2019. https://www.americamagazine.org/faith/2019/02/22/christian-belief-requires-transformation-not-facile-compromise.

Ivens, Michael, SJ. *Keeping in Touch: Posthumous Papers on Ignatian Topics*. Herefordshire: Gracewing, 2007.

Jacobs, Jane. *The Death and Life of Great American Cities*. New York: Vintage, 1961, 1992.

Jennings, Willie James. *Acts*. Louisville: Westminster John Knox, 2017.

Jewett, Robert. *Romans*. Hermeneia: A Critical and Historical Commentary on the Bible. Minneapolis: Fortress, 2007.

Johnson, Elizabeth A. *Friends of God and Prophets: A Feminist Theological Reading of the Communion of Saints*. New York: Continuum, 1998.

Kamudzandu, Israel. *Abraham our Father: Paul and the Ancestors in Postcolonial Africa*. Minneapolis: Fortress, 2013.

Katongole, Emmanuel. *Born from Lament: The Theology and Politics of Hope in Africa*. Grand Rapids: Eerdmans, 2017.

———. *The Journey of Reconciliation: Groaning for a New Creation in Africa*. Maryknoll, NY: Orbis, 2017.

———. "A Kairos Moment: Prophecy and Hope in the time of COVID-19." Keough School of Global Affairs, 2020.

———. *Who are My People? Love, Violence, and Christianity in Sub-Saharan Africa*. South Bend, IN: University of Notre Dame Press, 2022.

Katongole, Emmanuel, and Chris Rice. *Reconciling All Things: A Christian Vision for Justice, Peace and Healing*. Downers Grove, IL: InterVarsity, 2008.

Kelly, Jacques, and Erica L. Green. "Allan Tibbels, 1955–2010, Agent for Change in the City." *The Baltimore Sun*, Friday, June 4, 2010.

Keesmaat, Sylvia C. "Colossians and Ephesians." *The New Cambridge Companion to St. Paul*, edited by Bruce W. Longenecker, 135–51. Cambridge: Cambridge University Press, 2020.

Further Resources / Bibliography

Keesmaat, Sylvia C., and Brian J. Walsh. *Romans Disarmed: Resisting Empire, Demanding Justice*. Grand Rapids: Brazos, 2019.

Keller, Timothy. *Generous Justice: How Grace Makes Us Just*. New York: Penguin, 2010.

———. *Hope in Times of Fear: The Resurrection and Meaning of Easter*. New York: Viking, 2021.

Khalid, S. M. "Neighborhood Celebrates New Use for Old Convent." *The Sun*, Monday, November 12, 1990.

Kiess, John. "Common Ruins of Love: Augustine and the Politics of Meaning," in *Augustine and Social Justice*, edited by Teresa Delgado, John Doody, Kim Paffenrith, 207–26 Lanham, MD: Lexington, 2005.

Kilroe, Stephanie. *Anne Hope: The Struggle for Freedom, the Life of the Visionary Co-founder of Training for Transformation*. London: Darton, Longman, and Todd, 2019.

K'Meyer, Tracy E. *Interracialism and Christian Community in the Postwar South: The Story of Koinoina Farm*. Charlottesville: University of Virginia Press, 1997.

King, Martin Luther, Jr. *A Testament of Hope: The Essential Writings of Martin Luther King, Jr.* Edited by James M. Washington. San Francisco: Harper & Row, 1986.

Klinenberg, Eric. *Palaces for the People: How Social Infrastructure Can Help Fight Inequality, Polarization and the Decline of Civic Life*. New York: Crown, 2018.

Kloppenborg, John S. *Christ's Associations: Connecting and Belonging in the Ancient City*. New Haven: Yale University Press, 2019.

Kreider, Alan. *The Patient Ferment of the Early Church: The Improbable Rise of Christianity in the Roman Empire*. Grand Rapids: Baker Academic, 2016.

Lanahan, Lawrence. *The Lines Between Us: Two Families and a Quest to Cross Baltimore's Racial Divide*. New York: The New Press, 2019.

Lash, Nicholas. *Believing Three Ways in One God, A Reading of the Apostles Creed*. Notre Dame: University of Notre Dame Press, 1993.

Last, Richard. "Christ Worship in the Neighborhood." *New Testament Studies* 68 (2022) 310–25.

Lederach, John Paul, and Angela Jill Lederach. *When Blood and Bones Cry Out: Journeys Through the Soundscape of Healing and Reconciliation*. New York: Oxford University Press, 2010.

Lee, Michael E. *Revolutionary Saint: The Theological Legacy of Oscar Romero*. Maryknoll, NY: Orbis, 2018.

Lernoux, Penny, with Arthur Jones and Robert Ellsberg. *Hearts on Fire: The Story of the Maryknoll Sisters*. Maryknoll, NY: Orbis, 1993, 2012.

Levy, Ariel. "The Poetry of Systems." *The New Yorker*, December 18 and 25, 2017, 60–71.

Lincoln, C. Eric, and Lawrence Mamiya. *The Black Church in the African American Experience*. Durham, NC: Duke University Press, 1990.

Lohfink, Gerhard. *Jesus and Community: The Social Dimension of Christian Faith*. Translated by John P. Galvin. Philadelphia: Fortress, 1984.

Loughery, John, and Blythe Randolph. *Dorothy Day: Dissenting Voice of the American Century*. New York: Simon and Schuster, 2020.

Lowery, Wesley. *"They Can't Kill Us All": Ferguson, Baltimore, and a New Era in America's Racial Justice Movement*. New York: Little, Brown and Company, 2016.

MacFarquhar, Larissa. *Strangers Drowning: Grappling with Impossible Idealism, Drastic Choices, and the Overpowering Urge to Help*. New York: Penguin, 2015

MacGillis, Alec. "The Third Rail." *Places Journal*, March 2016. https://placesjournal.org/article/the-third-rail/?cn-reloaded=1.

Further Resources / Bibliography

Marsh, Charles. *The Beloved Community: How Faith Shapes Social Justice, From the Civil Rights Movement to Today.* New York: Basic Books, 2005.
———. *God's Long Summer: Stories of Faith and Civil Rights.* Princeton: Princeton University Press, 1997.
———. *Strange Glory: A Life of Dietrich Bonhoeffer.* New York: Alfred A. Knopf, 2014.
Marsh, Charles, Peter Slade, and Sarah Azaransky, eds. *Lived Theology: New Perspectives on Method, Style, and Pedagogy.* New York: Oxford University Press, 2016.
Martin, James, SJ. *The Jesuit Guide to Almost Everything: A Spirituality for Real Life.* New York: HarperOne, 2010.
Mavrodes, George I. *The Salvation of Zachary Baumkletter.* Downers Grove, IL: InterVarsity Fellowship, 1976.
Mbiti, John. *New Testament Eschatology in African Background.* Oxford: Oxford University Press, 1971.
McCaulley, Esau. *Reading While Black: African American Biblical Interpretation as an Exercise in Hope.* Downers Grove, IL: InterVarsity, 2020.
McDougall, Harold A. *Black Baltimore: A New Theory of Community.* Philadelphia: Temple University Press, 1993.
McElwee, Joshua. "Berrigan's Message to Peacemakers: Persevere." *National Catholic Reporter*, December 8, 2010. https://www.ncronline.org/berrigans-message-peacemakers-persevere.
McGhee, Heather. *The Sum of Us: What Racism Costs Everyone and How We Can Prosper Together.* New York: One World, 2021.
McKnight, John, and Peter Block. *The Abundant Community: Awakening the Power of Families and Neighborhoods.* San Francisco: Berrett-Koehler, 2010.
McLaren, Duncan, and Julian Agyeman. *Sharing Cities: A Case for Truly Smart and Sustainable Cities.* Cambridge: The MIT Press, 2015.
Meeks, Wayne A. *The First Urban Christians: The Social World of the Apostle Paul.* New Haven: Yale University Press, 1983.
Meggitt, Justin J. *Paul. Poverty and Survival.* Edinburgh: T&T Clark, 1998.
Merton, Thomas. *Faith and Violence: Christian Teaching and Christian Practice.* Notre Dame: University of Notre Dame Press, 1968.
Moltmann, Jürgen. *The Crucified God: The Cross of Christ as the Foundation and Criticism of Christian Theology.* Minneapolis: Fortress, 1991.
———. "The Liberation of Oppressors." *Journal of Theology for Southern Africa* 26 (1979) 24–37.
———. *In the End—the Beginning: The Life of Hope.* Minneapolis: Fortress, 2004.
———. *The Open Church: Invitation to a Messianic Lifestyle.* London: SCM, 1978.
———. *Resurrection to Eternal Life: On Dying and Rising.* Minneapolis: Fortress, 2021.
———. *The Source of Life: The Holy Spirit and the Theology of Life.* Minneapolis: Fortress, 1997.
———. *A Theology of Hope.* Minneapolis: Fortress, 1993.
Moore, Wes, with Erica L. Green. *Five Days: The Fiery Reckoning of an American City.* New York: One World, 2020.
Morgan, Teresa. *Roman Faith and Christian Faith.* Oxford: Oxford University Press, 2015.
Mouw, Richard J. *When the Kings Come Marching In: Isaiah and the New Jerusalem.* Grand Rapids: Eerdmans, 1983.
Myers, Ched. *Binding the Strong Man: A Political Reading of Mark's Story of Jesus.* Maryknoll, NY: Orbis, 1988.

Further Resources / Bibliography

Nouwen, Henri J. M. *Gracias! A Latin American Journal*. Maryknoll, NY: Orbis, 1983, 1993.

———. *The Inner Voice of Love: A Journey Through Anguish to Freedom*. New York: Image, 1996.

O'Connor, Kathleen M. *Jeremiah: Pain and Promise*. Minneapolis: Fortress, 2012.

O'Donovan, Oliver. *Entering into Rest: Ethics as Theology*, vol. 3. Grand Rapids: Eerdmans, 2017.

Ogden, Laura A. *Loss and Wonder at the World's End*. Durham, NC: Duke University Press, 2021.

O'Gorman, Frances. "Recreating Relationships: Some Insights from the Experiences of Base Communities in Brazil." *Transformation* 3:3 (1986) 12–16.

O'Halloran, James, SDB. *Living Cells: Vision and Practicalities of Small Christian Communities and Groups*. Dublin: Columba, 2010.

Parsons, Preston. "A Friendship for Others: Bonhoeffer and Bethge on the Theology and Practice of Friendship." PhD thesis, University of Cambridge, 2017.

Perkins, John. *Let Justice Roll Down*. Ventura, CA: Regal, 1976.

———. *One Blood: Parting Words to the Church on Race*. Chicago: Moody, 2018.

———. *A Quiet Revolution: The Christian Response to Human Need . . . A Strategy for Today*. Waco, TX: Word, 1976.

———. *With Justice for All*. Ventura, CA: Regal, 1982.

Perkins, John, with Karen Waddles. *Count it All Joy: The Ridiculous Paradox of Suffering*, Chicago: Moody, 2021.

———. *He Calls Me Friend: The Healing Power of Friendship in a Lonely World*. Chicago: Moody, 2019.

Paulsell, Stephanie. "The Strange Stuff: Reading Toni Morrison at Advent." *Christian Century*, December 18, 2019. https://www.christiancentury.org/article/faith-matters/reading-toni-morrison-advent.

Pietila, Antero. *Not in My Neighborhood: How Bigotry Shaped a Great American City*. Chicago: Ivan R. Dee, 2010.

Pohl, Christine D. *Living into Community: Cultivating the Practices that Sustain Us*. Grand Rapids: Eerdmans, 2012.

Polter, Julie. "Reviving Our Common Life in a World Struggling to Breathe." *Sojourners*, August 2020. https://sojo.net/magazine/august-2020/reviving-our-common-life-world-struggling-breathe.

Price, Peter B. *Seeds of the Word: Biblical Reflections for Small Church Communities*. London: Darton, Longman and Todd, 1996.

———. *A Shaking Reality: Daily Reflections for Advent*. London: Darton, Longman and Todd, 2018.

Quash, Ben. *Abiding*. London: Bloomsbury, 2013.

Quiros, Ansley. *God With Us: Lived Theology and the Freedom Struggle in Americus, Georgia, 1942–1976*. Chapel Hill: University of North Carolina Press, 2018.

Raboteau, Albert J. "American Salvation: The Place of Christianity in Public Life." *Boston Review*, April 4, 2005. https://www.bostonreview.net/articles/american-salvation-albert-raboteau-christianity-in-public-life/.

———. *Slave Religion: The "Invisible Institution" in the Antebellum South*. New York: Oxford University Press, 1978.

Radcliffe, Timothy. *Alive in God: A Christian Imagination*. London: Bloomsbury Continuum, 2019.

Further Resources / Bibliography

———. "On Finding Hope and Forgiveness in a Time of Hardship." *The Tablet*, July 13, 2022. https://www.thetablet.co.uk/features/2/22079/timothy-radcliffe-op-on-finding-hope-and-forgiveness-in-a-time-of-hardship.

———. "Shaped by Tenderness, the Most Beautiful Thing on Earth. *The Tablet*, February 2, 2023.https://www.thetablet.co.uk/features/2/22773/shaped-by-tenderness-the-most-beautiful-thing-on-earth.

Rauch, Henry. "Man in the Street: George Winchester." *The Sun*, July 10, 1950.

Robert, Dana L. *Faithful Friendships: Embracing Diversity in Christian Community*. Grand Rapids: Eerdmans, 2019.

Robinson, Marilynne. *The Death of Adam*. New York: Picador, 2005.

———. *Gilead*. New York: Farrar, Straus and Giroux, 2004.

———. *Jack*. New York: Farrar, Straus and Giroux, 2020.

———. *When I Was a Child I Read Books*. New York: Farrar, Straus and Giroux, 2012.

Rohr, Richard. *Job and the Mystery of Suffering: Spiritual Reflections*. New York: Crossroad, 1996.

Romero, Oscar. *The Violence of Love: The Pastoral Wisdom of Archbishop Oscar Romero*. Compiled and translated by James R. Brockman. Foreword by Henri J. M. Nouwen. San Francisco: Harper and Row, 1988.

Rothstein, Richard. *The Color of Law: A Forgotten History of How Our Government Segregated America*. New York: Liveright, 2017.

Rowe, G. Kavin. *Christianity's Surprise: A Sure and Certain Hope*. Nashville: Abingdon, 2020.

Ryon, Roderick N. *West Baltimore Neighborhoods: Sketches of Their History, 1840–1960*. Baltimore: The University of Baltimore Press, 1993.

Saint, Steve. "Nate Saint, Jim Elliott, Roger Youderian, Ed McCully and Peter Fleming: Cloud of Witnesses." In *Martyrs: Contemporary Writers on Modern Lives of Faith*, edited by Susan Bergman, 142–54. New York: HarperSanFrancisco, 1996.

Saint-Jean, Patrick, SJ. *The Crucible of Racism: Ignatian Spirituality and the Power of Hope*. Maryknoll, NY: Orbis, 2022.

Sanchez, Michelle Chaplin. *Calvin and the Resignification of the World: Creation, Incarnation, and the Problem of Political Theology in the 1559 Institutes*. Cambridge: Cambridge University Press, 2019.

Saperstein, Saundra. "Sandtown Typical of Urban Blight." *Washington Post*, July 2, 1980.

Scharen, Christian. "Learning Ministry Over Time: Embodying Practical Wisdom." In *For Life Abundant: Practical Theology, Theological Education, and Christian Ministry*, edited by Dorothy C. Bass and Craig Dykstra, 265–88. Grand Rapids: Eerdmans 2008.

Scherz, China. *Having People, Having Heart: Charity, Sustainable Development, and Problems of Dependence in Central Uganda*. Chicago: University of Chicago Press, 2014.

Schmemann, Alexander. *The Journals of Father Alexander Schmemann, 1973–1983*. Translated by Juliana Schmemann. Crestwood, NY: St. Vladimir's Seminary Press, 2000.

Schreiter, Robert J. *Constructing Local Theologies*. Maryknoll, NY: Orbis, 1995.

Sharp, Isaac B. *The Other Evangelicals: A Story of Liberal, Black, Progressive, Feminist, and Gay Christians—and the Movement that Pushed them Out*. Grand Rapids: Eerdmans 2023.

Further Resources / Bibliography

Sharpe, Christina. *In the Wake: On Blackness and Being*. Durham, NC: Duke University Press, 2016.

Shelby, Tommie. *The Idea of Prison Abolition*. Princeton: Princeton University Press, 2022.

Shelby, Tommie, and Brandon M. Terry, eds. *To Shape a New World: Essays on the Political Philosophy of Martin Luther King, Jr.* Cambridge: The Belknap Press of Harvard University Press, 2018.

Shelton, Taylor. "Rethinking the RECAP: Mapping the relational geographies of concentrated poverty and affluence in Lexington, Kentucky." *Urban Geography* 39:7 (2018) 1070–91.

Shenk, Wilbert R. "The Whole is Greater Than the Sum of the Parts: Moving Beyond Word and Deed." *Missiology: An International Review* 21:1 (1993) 65–75.

Shepard, Cassim. *City Makers: The Culture and Craft of Practical Urbanism*. New York: Monacelli, 2017.

Siegel, Eric. "Small School's Big Success." *The Sun*, January 24, 1997.

Smith, James K. A. *How To Inhabit Time: Understanding the Past, Facing the Future, Living Faithfully Now*. Grand Rapids: Brazos, 2022.

Smith, Kyle. *Cult of the Dead: A Brief History of Christianity*. Oakland: University of California Press, 2022.

Smith, Zadie. *Intimations: Six Essays*. New York: Penguin, 2020.

Snyder, Howard A. *The Community of the King*. 2nd ed. Downers Grove, IL: InterVarsity, 2004.

———. *Liberating the Church: The Ecology of Church and Kingdom*. Downers Grove, IL: InterVarsity, 1983.

Soelle, Dorothee. *The Silent Cry: Mysticism and Resistance*. Translated by Barbara and Martin Rumscheidt. Minneapolis: Fortress, 2001.

Soelle, Dorothee, with Shirley A. Cloyes. *To Work and to Love: A Theology of Creation*. Philadelphia: Fortress, 1984.

Spillers, Hortense Jeanette. "Fabrics of History: Essay on the Black Sermon." PhD diss., Brandeis University, 1974.

Stevenson, Bryan. *Just Mercy: A Story of Justice and Redemption*. New York: Spiegel and Grau, 2014.

Stoller, Paul. *Adventures in Blogging: Public Anthropology and Popular Media*. Toronto: Toronto University Press, 2018.

Stott, John. *God's New Society: The Message of Ephesians*, Downers Grove, IL: InterVarsity, 1979.

Stringfellow, William. *An Ethic for Christians and Other Aliens in a Strange Land*. Waco, TX: Word, 1976.

———. *Free in Obedience: The Radical Christian Life*. New York: Seabury, 1964.

———. *Instead of Death*. New and expanded ed. New York: Seabury, 1977.

———. *My People is the Enemy: An Autobiographical Polemic*. New York: Holt, Rinehart and Winston, 1964.

———. *A Simplicity of Faith: My Experience in Mourning*. Nashville: Abingdon, 1982.

Stringfellow, William, and Bill Wylie-Kellerman. *William Stringfellow: Essential Writings*. Maryknoll, NY: Orbis, 2013.

Swartz, David W. *Moral Minority: The Evangelical Left in an Age of Conservatism*. Philadelphia: University of Pennsylvania Press, 2012.

Swinton, John. *Becoming Friends of Time: Disability, Timefullness, and Discipleship*. Waco, TX: Baylor University Press, 2016.

Further Resources / Bibliography

Taylor, Charles. *A Secular Age.* Cambridge: The Belknap Press of Harvard University Press, 2007.

Taylor, Keeanga-Yamahtta. *Race for Profit: How Banks and the Real Estate Industry Undermined Black Homeownership.* Chapel Hill: University of North Carolina Press, 2019.

Thurman, Howard. *Disciplines of the Spirit.* Richmond, IN: Friends United, 1963.

———. *Jesus and the Disinherited.* Boston: Beacon, 1996.

Tisby, Jemar. *The Color of Compromise: The Truth About the American Church's Complicity in Racism.* Grand Rapids: Zondervan, 2019.

Thomas, Bettye Collier. *Jesus, Jobs, and Justice: African American Women and Religion.* New York: Knopf, 2010.

Tran, Jonathan. *Asian Americans and the Spirit of Racial Capitalism.* New York: Oxford University Press, 2021.

VanderWeele, Tyler J. "On the Promotion of Human Flourishing." *PNAS* 114:31 (August 1, 2017) 8148–56.

Vergara, Camilo José. *American Ruins.* New York: Monacelli, 1999.

———. *Detroit is No Dry Bones: The Eternal City of the Industrial Age.* Ann Arbor: University of Michigan Press, 2016.

Valiente, O. Ernesto. *Liberation Through Reconciliation: Jon Sobrino's Christological Spirituality.* New York: Fordham University Press, 2016.

Villarosa, Linda. *Under the Skin: The Hidden Toll of Racism on American Lives and on the Health of our Nation.* New York: Doubleday, 2022.

Volf, Miroslav. *The End of Memory: Remembering Rightly in a Violent World.* Grand Rapids: Eerdmans, 2006.

———. *Exclusion and Embrace: A Theological Exploration of Identity, Otherness and Reconciliation.* Nashville: Abingdon, 1996.

Volf, Miroslav, and Ryan McAnnally-Linz. *The Home of God: A Brief Story of Everything.* Grand Rapids: Brazos, 2022.

Wadell, Paul C. *Becoming Friends: Worship, Justice, and the Practice of Christian Friendship.* Grand Rapids: Brazos, 2002.

———. *Friendship and the Moral Life.* Notre Dame: University of Notre Dame Press, 1989.

Wallis, Jim. *Agenda for Biblical People.* San Francisco: Harper & Row, 1976.

———. *The Call to Conversion.* San Francisco: Harper & Row, 1981.

Walls, Andrew. *The Cross Cultural Process in Christian History: Studies in the Transmission and Appropriation of Faith.* Maryknoll, NY: Orbis, 2002.

———. *The Missionary Movement in Christian History: Studies in the Transmission of Faith.* Maryknoll, NY: Orbis, 1996.

Walsh, Brendan, and Willa Bickham. *The Long Loneliness in Baltimore: Stories Along the Way.* Baltimore: Apprentice House, 2016.

West, Cornel. *Prophesy Deliverance! An Afro-American Revolutionary Christianity.* Philadelphia: Westminster, 1982.

———. *Prophetic Fragments.* Grand Rapids: Eerdmans/Trenton, NJ: Africa World, 1988.

Wilkerson, Isabel. *Caste: The Origins of our Discontents.* New York: Random House, 2020.

———. *The Warmth of Other Suns: The Epic Story of America's Great Migration.* New York: Random House, 2010.

Williams, Delores S. *Sisters in the Wilderness: The Challenge of Womanist God-Talk.* Maryknoll, NY: Orbis, 1993.

Further Resources / Bibliography

Williams, Rowan. *Christ the Heart of Creation*. London: Bloomsbury Continuum, 2018.

———. "The Christian Priest Today: Lecture on the Occasion of the 150th Anniversary of Ripon College." http://rowanwilliams.archbishopofcanterbury.org/articles.php/2097/the-christian-priest-today-lecture-on-the-occasion-of-the-150th-anniversary-of-ripon-college-cuddesd.html.

———. *Luminaries: Twenty Lives That Illuminate the Christian Way*. London: SPCK, 2019.

———. "On William Stringfellow." Unpublished lecture at the Church of St. Edward the Martyr, New York City, 2017.

———. "Religious Lives." In *Faith in the Public Square*, 313–25. London: Bloomsbury, 2012.

———. *Tokens of Trust: An Introduction to Christian Belief*. Louisville: Westminster John Knox, 2007.

———. *The Tragic Imagination*. Oxford: Oxford University Press, 2016.

———. *The Way of St. Benedict*. London: Bloomsbury Continuum, 2020.

Wilson, William Julius. *When Work Disappears: The World of the New Urban Poor*. New York: Knopf, 1996.

Winner, Lauren F. *The Dangers of Christian Practice: On Wayward Gifts, Characteristic Damage, and Sin*. New Haven: Yale University Press, 2017.

Wink, Walter. *My Struggle to Become Human*. Minneapolis: Fortress, 2018.

Winston, Diane. *Righting the American Dream: How the Media Mainstreamed Reagan's Evangelical Vision*. Chicago: The University of Chicago Press, 2023.

Winter, Gibson. *The Suburban Captivity of the Churches: An Analysis of Protestant Responsibility in the Expanding Metropolis*. New York: Doubleday, 1961.

Wolterstorff, Nicholas. *Hearing the Call: Liturgy, Justice, Church and World*. Edited by Mark R. Gornik and Gregory Thompson. Grand Rapids, Eerdmans 2011.

———. *In This World of Wonders: Memoir of a Life in Learning*. Grand Rapids: Eerdmans, 2019.

———. *Justice: Rights and Wrongs*. Princeton: Princeton University Press, 2008.

———. "Spirituality, Justice, and Remembering." *The Covenant Quarterly* 70:1–2 (2012) 10–20.

———. *Until Justice and Peace Embrace*. Grand Rapids: Eerdmans, 1983.

Wright, N. T. *Paul and the Faithfulness of God*. 2 vols. Minneapolis: Fortress, 2013.

———. *Surprised by Hope: Rethinking Heaven, the Resurrection, and the Mission of the Church*. New York: Harper One, 2008.

Wylie-Kellermann, Bill. *Celebrant's Flame: Daniel Berrigan in Memory and Reflection*. Eugene, OR: Cascade, 2021.

Young, Frances M. *Brokenness and Blessing: Towards a Biblical Spirituality*. Grand Rapids: Baker, 2007.

Young, Frances, and David F. Ford. *Meaning and Truth in 2 Corinthians*. London: SPCK, 1997.

Zournazi, Mary, and Rowan Williams. *Justice and Love: A Philosophical Dialogue*. London: Bloomsbury Academic, 2021.

Christ is all that's left, if you're looking for a mystery.
He's real as a man.
Don't just stand there! Sit him down. Offer him some bread!
He'll understand that; bread comes across.
So does Christ—Luke says so—in the breaking of bread.
What a beautiful sound—try and see!

—Daniel Berrigan, *Love, Love at the End*

www.ingramcontent.com/pod-product-compliance
Lightning Source LLC
Chambersburg PA
CBHW061940220426
43662CB00012B/1978